O9-BTO-406

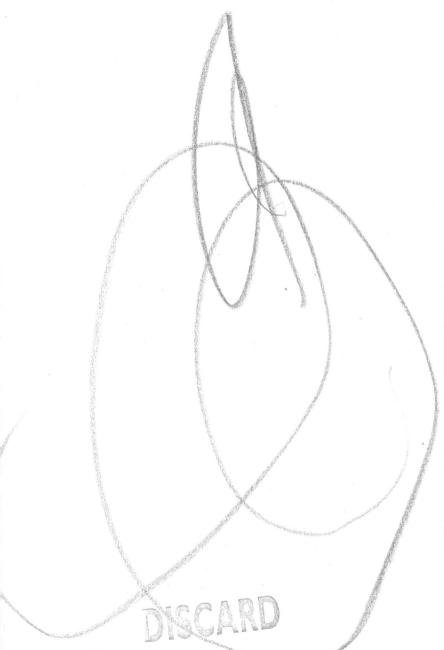

INTRODUCTION TO
TOLSTOY'S WRITINGS

INTRODUCTION

TO

TOLSTOY'S

WRITINGS

BY

ERNEST J. SIMMONS

The University of Chicago Press

CHICAGO AND LONDON

Library of Congress Catalog Card Number: 67-30427

THE UNIVERSITY OF CHICAGO PRESS, CHICAGO & LONDON
The University of Toronto Press, Toronto 5, Canada

PREFACE

During the last twenty years I have published a considerable
number of items on Tolstoy's life and on his separate works.
A friend, familiar with the bulk of this varied material, suggested that I carve out of it a kind of guide to introduce
students and interested readers in general to the writings of
Leo Tolstoy. The proposal was attractive as one that would
enable me to impose organization and thus a sense of development on a favorite subject which I had never previously studied
as a connected whole.

Any sensible idea of this sort, the execution of which seems
so easy at first sight, soon turns into a rugged and time-consum-
ing experience of hard choices in design, inclusions and exclu-
sions, revisions, and bringing up to date. What has emerged
is a book—consisting in large measure of a selection of material
from my published works—that attempts to describe and discuss all those writings of Tolstoy which appear to have enduring significance. With few exceptions, they are works that have
been translated into English. His fiction and plays have been

considered with some regard for chronological order in an effort to trace Tolstoy's development as a creative artist. But I have also included treatments of major non-literary works in order to show his concurrent development as a thinker and reformer in such diverse fields as education, religious thought, aesthetics, and social, political, and moral problems. For these writings, so often ignored, are intrinsically important; they are also a tangible part of his total literary experience, and they enable us to evaluate his position as a leading thinker of the nineteenth century, one whose ideas have not lost their significance for us today.

The book is not intended for scholarly specialists on Tolstoy, though they might gain some insights here and there from its pages, nor does it pretend to offer studies in higher criticism of his famous novels. The effort is what its title indicates—an introduction to the writings of Tolstoy for those readers who wish initially to find their way among his voluminous works. Nowadays we are used to political biographies of great leaders of governments; this book, in a sense, is a brief literary biography or, more precisely, the biography of the literary career of one of the world's greatest novelists and thinkers.

Permissions to make use of the following published works are hereby acknowledged:

(In the Introduction and Chapters IV, V, XII): Selections from Chapter IV, "Tolstoy," *Introduction to Russian Realism. Pushkin, Gogol, Dostoevsky, Tolstoy, Chekhov, Sholokhov*, by Ernest J. Simmons. Copyright 1965 by Indiana University Press. Reprinted by permission of Indiana University Press.

(In Chapter I): Selection from the Introduction by Ernest J. Simmons to *Nikolenka's Childhood*, by Leo Tolstoy. Copyright 1963 by Maurice Sendak. Reprinted from *Nikolenka's Childhood*, by Leo Tolstoy, by permission of Pantheon Books, a Division of Random House, Inc.

(In Chapter I): Selections from the Introduction by Ernest J. Simmons to *Leo Tolstoy: Short Stories* Vol. I (ML-346). Copyright 1964 by Random House, Inc. Reprinted from *Leo Tolstoy: Short Stories* Vol. I, by permission.

(In Chapter II): Selections from the Introduction by Ernest J. Simmons to *Short Novels* Vol. I, by Leo Tolstoy (ML-354). Copyright 1965 by Random House, Inc. Reprinted from *Short Novels* Vol. I, by Leo Tolstoy, by permission.

(In Chapters III, VI, VII, X): Selections from *Leo Tolstoy* by Ernest J. Simmons. Copyright 1946 by Ernest J. Simmons. Reprinted by permission of Atlantic-Little, Brown and Company, Publishers.

(In Chapter VI): Selections from the Introduction by Ernest J. Simmons to *Selected Essays*, by Leo Tolstoy (ML-347). Copyright 1964 by Random House, Inc. Reprinted from *Selected Essays*, by Leo Tolstoy, by permission.

(In Chapter VIII): Selections from the Introduction by Ernest J. Simmons to *Leo Tolstoy: Short Stories* Vol. II (ML-361). Copyright 1965 by Random House, Inc. Reprinted from *Leo Tolstoy: Short Stories* Vol. II, by permission.

(In Chapter IX): Selections from the Introduction by Ernest J. Simmons to *Short Novels* Vol. II, by Leo Tolstoy (ML-367). Copyright 1966 by Random House, Inc. Reprinted from *Short Novels* Vol. II, by Leo Tolstoy, by permission.

(In Chapter XI): Introduction by Ernest J. Simmons. Copyright 1963 by George Macy Companies, Inc.; reprinted from their edition of *Resurrection* by Leo Tolstoy, by arrangement with The Limited Editions and Heritage Clubs.

(In Chapter XII): Selections from "Tolstoy and the Kremlin," by Ernest J. Simmons, *The Atlantic Monthly*, October 1960, by permission of The Atlantic Monthly Company.

It should be pointed out that this reprinted material has been subjected to thorough revision in every case. Many deletions have been made and not a few additions. In a number of the chapters fresh material has been introduced.

With very few exceptions, all quotations from the literary works of Tolstoy have been taken, with previous permission, from the excellent translations by Louise and Aylmer Maude in *Tolstoy Centenary Edition* (21 vols.; London: Oxford University Press, 1928–37.

All other translations, from Tolstoy's diaries and letters and from numerous Russian sources, are my own and were originally done in connection with my biography, *Leo Tolstoy* (Boston: Little, Brown and Company, 1946).

During the final stages of the preparation of this book, I served as Acting Director of The Center for Advanced Studies, Wesleyan University. I am deeply indebted to the Center for allowing me substantial free time from administrative duties to work on *Introduction to Tolstoy's Writings*, as well as for the use of its research and secretarial services. In particular, I offer my profound thanks to Mrs. Tania Senff for her many kindnesses and her expert typing of the manuscript.

E. J. S.

CONTENTS

INTRODUCTION

I

Much has been written about similarities and dissimilarities in Dostoevsky and Tolstoy, but no two great novelists differed so fundamentally in their conception and practice of realism in the art of fiction. Though both authors, ideologically speaking, had a vested interest in Christ's teachings, Dostoevsky was peculiarly spiritual and Tolstoy completely earthbound.

Like Gogol, whom he preferred as a storyteller, Tolstoy believed that a work, in order to be good, must come singing from the author's soul. But he criticized Gogol for a pitiless and unloving attitude to his characters, a charge from which he absolved Dickens, and he could quite justly have absolved himself. Though in *What is Art?* he failed to admit any of Dostoevsky's writings to his category of "universal art," which conveys feelings of common life accessible to everyone, he did include the tales of Pushkin and Gogol.

Early in his artistic development Tolstoy had the greatest admiration for Pushkin, although he complained of the bareness of his prose and criticized *The Captain's Daughter* because the interest in events predominates over interest in details of feeling. But the account is well known, although its veracity has been questioned, of how his enthusiasm for the opening of a Pushkin short story, which plunged directly into the action, inspired him to begin *Anna Karenina* in the same manner.

The derivation of Tolstoy's fiction from the classical school of Russian realism begun by Pushkin can hardly be doubted. However, this colossus of a genius, who took all knowledge for his province, read omnivorously in foreign literatures as well as in Russian, and one may trace in the rich unrolling tapestry of his art threads from the works of English eighteenth-century writers, especially Sterne, and, in the nineteenth century, Thackeray and Dickens, whom he regarded as the greatest novelist of the age, and also from the French realists, particularly Stendhal. If literature is the memory of culture, Tolstoy seems to have remembered it all, but so original was his artistic nature that anything he may have borrowed he completely assimilated and made his own. The realistic tradition he inherited he greatly expanded and enriched in practice so that the finished product became the despair of imitators.

No novelist was more acutely aware of the reality around him than Tolstoy or more exhaustively absorbed, through the intellect and senses, in all its manifestations. Unlike Dostoevsky, who creates a world of his own in the image of the real world, Tolstoy accepts the real world, and his picture of it is fresh and interesting because he sees so much more of it than his readers, but its commonplaces, observed through the prism of his imagination, take on new meaning. That is, he is able to perceive genuine poetry in the average which so often embodies the reality of man's dreams and hopes. Man needs hope as much or more than he needs knowledge, Tolstoy declared in answer to a speech of Zola who advised a group of French students to accept science as the road to a new faith rather than build their living faith on the debris of dead ones, for, he warned, reality becomes a school of perversion which must be killed or denied since it will lead to nothing but ugliness and crime. Tolstoy countered in his essay "Non-Acting": "It is commonly said that reality is that which exists, or that only what exists is real. Just the contrary is the case: true reality, that which we really know, is what has never existed."

That reality is so often different from what men and women hope and dream, that life often disappoints them because they have confused the imagined with the real, is a central problem with Tolstoy's more reflective characters. In *The Cossacks* Olenin's conception of the romantic existence of these people of the Caucasus is shattered by the reality of it; in *War and Peace* Prince Andrew's exaggerated notions of a career in the army and in politics are harshly corrected by experience; and in *Anna Karenina* Levin's idealistic hopes about marriage are soon disillusioned. In such cases Tolstoy usually demonstrates that the reality of things is richer, more affirmative and life-giving than the reality imagined by such characters. But he does this through their active experiences, although reflection plays its part, for he never forgets that realistic literature should portray human beings in action. Disillusionment with reality is not resolved in metaphysical quests, as in Dostoevsky's fiction and in that of not a few novelists today. Tolstoy's alienated man does not ask himself the everlasting question: Who am I? but rather: Why am I here and where am I going? At least the matter of self-identification is already resolved. The different emphasis is fundamental and it is a quality of Tolstoy's realism.

To those who knew him intimately, Tolstoy always gave the impression of a normal human being who enjoyed to the full the ordinary activities of society, but he combined with this normality what might be described as an abnormal intensity of sensibility and temperament. Even as a child his endless high spirits set him apart from others, and if he were petted tears of joy would come to his eyes. His sister remarked that as a boy he was like a ray of light and would dash into the room with a happy smile as if he wished to tell everyone of a new discovery he had just made. These unusual characteristics remained with him as a grown man and, along with his extraordinary faculty for intellectual analysis, enabled him to enter sympathetically into the feelings of every kind of person. In short, if he participated in the same pleasures and interests of the mass of mankind, he realized them more imaginatively and passionately. That is, Tolstoy's intense sensibility and temperament added a unique dimension to his creative process which enhances the men and women of his novels, as well as their experiences, with amazing life-affirming qualities. Though his novels excite the imagination and seem laden with significance, they achieve this without any sacrifice of probability. It is hard to think of any other great writer whose fiction was so closely bound up with fact. On the other hand, if his intellect and imagination were stimulated entirely by objective observation, Tolstoy's moral nature compelled him to be profoundly concerned with the state of the soul.

2

The great poet Pushkin, and not Tolstoy, stands as the brightest and foremost symbol of Russian literature in that country, very much as Shakespeare does in English literature. However, if Tolstoy is regarded not only as a literary artist but also as a religious philosopher and modern reformer, then he was possibly the greatest single moral force in the world in the second half of the nineteenth century. Certainly no Russian writer is better known outside his country than Tolstoy. Yet it is probably true that his various religious, moral, and philosophical works would never have received the wide hearing they did if

Tolstoy had not already been the author of *War and Peace* and *Anna Karenina*.

During his lifetime the tremendous popular impact of these novels and other purely literary works placed him at the head of all Russian writers. Even his two chief rivals acknowledged his supreme position. Dostoevsky, with his feeling of inferiority about Russian culture, joyfully hailed *Anna Karenina* as superior to any Western European novel in the nineteenth century. Turgenev, who could never get along with Tolstoy as a man and on one occasion narrowly avoided fighting a duel with him, profoundly admired his genius and on his deathbed pleaded with him, in the famous phrase, "great author of the Russian land," to return to writing belles-lettres.

By the last two decades of the nineteenth century what might be called the "saturation realism" of Tolstoy encountered a mixed reception in Western Europe. The current French naturalist dicta in criticism and perhaps also some of Tolstoy's extreme religious and moral views, which had begun to filter into the West, hindered an unprejudiced appreciation of his fiction. Upon reading a French translation of *War and Peace* in 1880, Flaubert wrote Turgenev: "It is of the first rank! What painting and what psychology! . . . It seemed to me at times that there were things worthy of Shakespeare! I uttered cries of admiration during the reading!"

In general, however, French critics compared Tolstoy's works, especially *Anna Karenina*, unfavorably with *Madame Bovary* with its impeccable form, tailored style, and naturalistic detail. Their tendency was to express bewilderment over the vast mass of reality reflected in Tolstoy's major novels and to regard them as peculiarly formless and artless—the chaotic outpourings of some super-reporter of experience. Nor did Matthew Arnold in England clarify the situation much by basing his preference of *Anna Karenina* over *Madame Bovary* partly on the conviction that Tolstoy's novel was not really a work of art at all but a piece of life, and that what it lost in art it gained in reality. And Henry James' nearsighted discovery of "large loose baggy monsters" in Tolstoy's fiction, his lament over the absence of "a deep-breathing economy of an organic form," and later E. M. Forster's comment on *War and Peace* as an "untidy book" have contributed to this notion of formlessness and artlessness which has clung to so much Western criticism of Tolstoy. In its application to serious fiction, Arnold's dichotomy of life and art is a spurious conception. Not "a piece of life" but life in all its manifestations crowds the huge canvas of Tolstoy's masterpieces. Their patterns of human relationships are always carefully planned, and plot is a poetic form reflecting reality rather than a contrived frame on which to stretch events. If the transformation of reality into art has been effected with equal skill in, let us say, Stendhal's *The Red and the Black* or Flaubert's *Madame Bovary*, in no novel has so *much* reality been transformed into art as in *War and Peace*.

In the Soviet Union, Tolstoy is venerated and his works have been published in millions of copies. The ninety-volume Jubilee Edition of all his writings is in completeness, textual accuracy, and scholarly annotation one of the most magnificent tributes ever paid to a great author. Soviet scholarship on Tolstoy is extremely copious and much of it of high quality, but where interpretation is required, it is more often than not dominated by Lenin's Marxian formulations, especially by his article, "Leo Tolstoy as a Mirror of the Russian Revolution." Lenin, more modest than Stalin as a literary critic, made the sharpest distinction between Tolstoy the artist, whom he praised in the highest terms, and Tolstoy the thinker, whose doctrines of moral perfectibility and nonresistance to evil he contemptuously dismissed. Lenin did laud Tolstoy's stubborn opposition to tsarist oppression and viewed such activities as an important factor in the developing revolutionary movement. Tolstoy, of course, abhorred the violence of revolution, and he once declared in his diary that "Socialists will never destroy poverty and the inequality of capacities. The strongest and most intelligent will always make use of the weaker and more stupid. . . . Even if that takes place which Marx predicted, then the only thing that will happen is that despotism will be passed on."

Such a statement, and others like it, have not discouraged Marxian investigations of Tolstoy's fiction. An outstanding one, illustrative of most in interpretation but differing from those of Soviet critics in the author's deep knowledge of Western European literature as well as Russian, was contributed by George Lukács, the brilliant Hungarian Marxist literary critic who spent a number of years in the Soviet Union. Despite his wide and illuminating frame of reference, Lukács, like Lenin, narrowly argues that Tolstoy created his literary masterpieces on the basis of an essentially false philosophy, but that as a political reactionary he unconsciously dramatized the revolutionary forces of his time. It is hard to imagine Tolstoy ever doing anything unconsciously, particularly in his writings. He would have agreed fully with Chekhov that nothing happens by chance in art.

In order to overcome the unpoetic nature of a society permeated by capitalism—Lukács maintains in his *Studies in European Realism*—Tolstoy makes the exploited peasant, either consciously or unconsciously, the central problem of his fiction. "The poetic starting-point in the presentation of each character by Tolstoy," Lukács writes, "was the question: in what way was their life based on the receipt of ground-rents and on the exploitation of the peasants and what problems did this social basis produce in their lives."

In these terms Anna Karenina's fatal passion for Vronsky becomes for Lukács another tragedy growing out of "the contradictions latently present . . . in every bourgeois love and marriage." Even the famous mowing scene in this novel, when viewed in terms of Levin's un-Marxian attitude toward the peasants, is set down as "a sentimental attitude to physical labor." In a review of *Anna Karenina*, Dostoevsky, unlike Lukács, censures Tolstoy for making the central problem of all his writing not the exploited peasantry, but the landed gentry. The ineptness of this kind of criticism is unwittingly limned by D. H. Lawrence in his poem: "Now It's Happened":

> But Tolstoy was a traitor
> to the Russia that needed him most,
> the clumsy, bewildered Russia
> so worried by the Holy Ghost.
> He shifted his job on to the peasants
> and landed them all on toast.

The vital point missed by Lukács is that Tolstoy, whenever he dwells upon man's inhumanity to man in his fiction, is never directly attacking a political system, but rather man in general for placing his own egotism ahead of the common needs of humanity. Even toward the end of his life, when he excoriated the tsar's government for its abuses, he was in effect denouncing all governments, whose disappearance he devoutly hoped for in terms of his doctrine of Christian anarchism. The radical democrats of the 1860's, such as Dobrolyubov and Chernyshevsky, and the revolutionists who followed were all profoundly distasteful to Tolstoy.

In appraising Tolstoy's attitude toward the peasant, one must make a sharp distinction between the first fifty years of his life, when most of his great fiction, including *War and Peace* and *Anna Karenina*, was written, and the remaining years after his spiritual upheaval. In the latter period it is true that he came to believe that just as a child is more perfect and closer to ideal harmony than the grown man, so is the simple peasant closer to it than self-destructive parasites of the elite. And in the end, shortly before his death, Tolstoy left his home to realize a dream of breaking with his privileges and settling with the toiling peasants whom he had come to regard as "the finest and most moral class of people in Russia."

But when he was writing the famous fiction on which Lukács bases his theorizing, Count Leo Tolstoy's instincts were entirely those of the aristocratic heritage that was his birthright. In fact, there is much reason to suppose that he never abandoned the confidence, refinement, and sense of authority of the landed gentry however much his later humanitarian convictions led him to advocate the cause of underprivileged workers and peasants.

Actually, peasants play a relatively small part in the total corpus of his fiction, and he rarely stresses their feelings of class opposition to the gentry. Anticipating the objections of readers of *War and Peace* to his concentration on members of his own class, he wrote in the draft of an unused foreword: "The lives of officials, merchants, seminarists, and peasants do not interest me and are only partly understandable to me; the lives of the aristocrats of that time, thanks to the documents of the period and other reasons, are understandable, interesting, and dear to me." He is more forthright on his prejudices in a note to himself in one of the draft versions of *War and Peace* where he flatly states that the lives of all people not in his own class, including peasants, seem boring and monotonous and that all their actions stem from the same motives: envy of their superiors, self-interest, and material passions. And he concludes: "I am an aristocrat because I cannot believe in the lofty intellect, the fine taste, or the complete honesty of a man who picks his nose and whose soul communicates with God."

I

LITERARY BEGINNINGS

Tolstoy started scribbling as a boy, and in his early diary, which he began at the age of eighteen and continued, with interruptions, throughout the remainder of his life, we may observe him serving an unconscious apprenticeship to the novelist's art of selection and analysis. In numerous entries dealing with his inner experiences as a youth, he reveals an intense interest in the suppressed motives of behavior. And his fondness for classifying all manner of human attributes in the diary suggests his later talent for conquering the subconscious by an application of penetrating understanding.

Certainly the transition from the kind of analysis in his youthful diary to that in his first piece of fiction, "A History of Yesterday" (1851), was a natural and easy one to make. The beginning of the narrative concerns an evening spent with distant relatives. Then, on his way home, the hero animadverts amusingly on drivers and carriages. Finally, as he drops off to sleep, he speculates on the problem of dreams. All this Tolstoy apparently intended to subordinate to the design of a larger work. It was an unusual performance for a beginner and it is unlike anything in Russian literature up to that time. Though it is a fragment, it is entirely self-contained and may readily be regarded as a completed short story. To the technique of delving into motivation, found in his diary, he has added the spice of Laurence Sterne's analytical method in the *Sentimental Journey*, which Tolstoy had been reading and part of which he later translated as an exercise in style. Sterne's influence is obvious in Tolstoy's concentration on peculiar details, in the posturings and digressions, in the analysis of conscious and subconscious thoughts and feelings of characters reacting to particular situations, and in the transformation of all the confused associations of thought that enter the hero's head as he falls asleep. The twenty-three-year-old Tolstoy revelled in his newly discovered powers of analysis, and it was a pity that he failed to go on with the work, but he never returned to this exuberant abandon in his fiction.

Perhaps one reason why Tolstoy did not continue "A History of Yesterday" is that shortly after starting it he set out on a long journey to the Caucasus with his brother Nicholas who was an army officer there. He had become dissatisfied with what he considered an idle and even debauched life on his estate at Yasnaya Polyana and in Moscow and Petersburg, and he believed that a radical change was essential. He remained in the Caucasus for more than two years, serving first as a volunteer, then as a cadet, in an artillery battery, and he distinguished himself in fighting bravely against the fierce hill tribes.

Along with his rugged army existence and the usual soldierly carousing, Tolstoy also led a life of the mind and literature. He read much, thought hard about various deep subjects, as his diary attests, and wrote a great deal. In fact, much of his initial literary period is closely associated with the Caucasus, for it was there that he finished his first published work, the autobiographical short novel *Childhood* (1852), began its sequel, *Boy-*

hood, wrote his short story "The Raid" (1852), and later three others which were based on his Caucasian experiences, and started several more tales and articles.

2

On July 3, 1852, the young Tolstoy wrote N. A. Nekrasov, distinguished poet and editor of the *Contemporary*, Russia's leading progressive magazine: "My request will cost you such little effort that I am sure you will not refuse to grant it. Look over this manuscript, and if it is not suitable for printing, return it to me. If you appraise it otherwise, tell me what it is worth in your opinion and print it in your magazine. I agree in advance to any cutting you may find necessary, but I desire that it be printed without additions or changes in the text." The future author of *War and Peace* and *Anna Karenina* then went on to add in his letter that the manuscript in question was the first part of a novel under the general title of "Four Epochs of Growth," and that the appearance of the latter parts would depend upon the success of the first. The letter concluded on a flattering note, no doubt prompted by his anxiety over the worth and soundness of his first sustained effort to write fiction: "I am convinced that an experienced and well-intentioned editor, especially in Russia, by virtue of his position as a constant intermediary between author and reader, can always indicate in advance the success of a work and the public reaction. Therefore, I await your answer with impatience. It will encourage me to continue a favorite occupation or oblige me to cease at the very beginning."

With this letter Tolstoy sent the manuscript of *Childhood*. The young author's painful uncertainty is understandable—he had not yet published a line. But very early in the morning, or late at night after a day of hunting, carousing, or activity with the battery, he worked away at *Childhood*. Occasionally, in his enthusiasm over a chapter, he would read it to his talented brother Nicholas, but he nearly always regretted these premature hearings.

It is instructive to follow the entries on *Childhood*, in Tolstoy's diary, during the period of writing, for they reveal the stern artistic demands he made upon himself even at the very outset of his literary career. Time and again he noted in the diary that the writing of the novel was going badly and the rewriting worse: "Without regret, I must destroy all unclear places, prolix, irrelevant, in a word, everything unsatisfactory, even though they may be fine in themselves." He cautioned himself to adhere to the rule that no addition, however talented, could improve a work as much as a deletion, and the four complete drafts of *Childhood* testify to his unswerving devotion to this injunction. He alternated between moods of deep satisfaction and utter despair, in which he began to doubt that he possessed any ability. "Have I talent comparable to that of recent Russian writers?" he asked himself in the diary and promptly answered: "Positively no." On the other hand, there were precious moments when he read over a particularly successful passage and then he imagined that genius must have prompted his pen: "I reread the chapter 'Grief,' and while so doing wept from my very heart."

Almost two months passed before Tolstoy received Nekrasov's reply, where he jotted down in his diary: "It drove me silly with joy." The famous editor had agreed to print *Childhood* in his periodical, and he added in the letter: "Not knowing the continuation, I cannot say definitely, but it seems to me that the author has talent. In any case, the author's bent and the simplicity and realism of the contents constitute the production's unquestionable worth." He concluded with a request for the continuation and a plea that the author reveal his name. (Tolstoy had signed the manuscript solely with the initials of his first name and patronymic—"L.N.").

When Tolstoy reminded the editor in a subsequent letter

that he had received no payment, Nekrasov coolly informed him that it was his practice not to offer an honorarium for an author's first work, but that he would pay him the best rates for any further manuscripts submitted. However, the wily Nekrasov took the precaution to soften this disappointment by adding that he had by now read the proof, believed it to be even better than when he had first read it in manuscript, and that he had absolutely no doubts about the author's talent.

Tolstoy received a published copy of *Childhood* at the end of October, but the beginner's pleasure at seeing his first work in print was not unmixed with annoyance over mutilations of both the censor and the editor. He hurried off a sharp note to Nekrasov, in which he scolded him for changing the title to *The Story of My Childhood*. Of what concern to anybody, he asked, was the story of *my* childhood? And he ridiculed a number of changes that had been made in the text against his express wish. In reading the published version, he declared, he underwent the feeling of a father who saw his child's hair hacked by an inexperienced barber. But he concluded his letter on a more cheerful note, accepting Nekrasov's generous financial offer for future works, and promising to send him another story when he had it ready.

Shortly after reading *Childhood* in print, Tolstoy went to a neighboring post to hunt with fellow officers. In a hut where they stopped to rest he came across an issue of *National Notes* which contained a highly appreciative review of his short novel. He eagerly read and reread the account, dwelling greedily on every note of praise. The reviewer's final judgment must have made his heart jump: "If this is the first production of L. N., then one ought to congratulate Russian literature on the appearance of a new and remarkable talent." Tears of joy filled the eyes of the impressionable young author, and he experienced a special thrill from the thought that the comrades sitting around him were not aware of the fact that it was he who was being lauded in such lofty terms.

This review and the news he soon received from relatives in Moscow and Petersburg, who were in on the secret of his authorship, concerning the enthusiastic reception of *Childhood* quickly dissipated Tolstoy's vexation over the editor's disfiguring of his brain child. On all sides readers raved about the novel and were curious to learn the author's real name. It was said that Panaev, co-editor of the *Contemporary*, was avoided by friends because he insisted upon cornering them on the street and reading extracts from the new work. Turgenev, already quite famous by that time, wrote Nekrasov urging him to encourage the unknown author and convey to him his greetings and praise. And Dostoevsky, in exile in far-off Siberia, wrote a friend to ask who was the mysterious L. N. whose recent work had so excited him. Hardly any young writer had knocked his head so violently against the stars of success with a first production as Tolstoy had done with *Childhood*.

Though *Childhood* is in the tradition of classical Russian realism begun by Pushkin, one can detect curious traces of foreign influences in the work. As in the case of "A History of Yesterday" certain aspects of the *Sentimental Journey*, especially Sterne's love of humanity and pervasive sensibility, as well as tricks of style, are clearly reflected in *Childhood*. In fact, in the several drafts of the work one can detect the care with which Tolstoy tried to eliminate the more obvious traces of this influence, but the final version still owes much to Sterne. Further, it is very likely that the *Bibliothèque de mon oncle* of the Swiss writer, R. Töpfer, may have inspired Tolstoy to write about childhood, although no direct traces of borrowing from this work are observable.

But in most respects this first short novel is a highly original work. Tolstoy once remarked: "When I wrote *Childhood* it seemed that no one before me had so felt and depicted all the charms and poetry of childhood." And this is an admirable brief description of the work, which is simply the story of a child's life up to the age of about fourteen. What especially impresses the reader is Tolstoy's wonderful skill in evoking childhood memories and associations that all have forgotten or only dimly remember, but which, when recalled with feeling, seem infallibly true and altogether delightful. If he criticized Pushkin's historical novel, *The Captain's Daughter*, because the interest in events predominates over the interest in feeling, it was precisely in the feelings of his characters that Tolstoy was primarily interested, and in the psychological reasons why they feel as they do. In the introductory statement to *Childhood*, he warns his readers that they must be understanding in order to appreciate his book, for he writes it from the heart, not from the head.

Of course, there is a great deal of Tolstoy's own childhood in this work, especially in the thoughts and feelings expressed by the central character, Nicholas. More so perhaps than that of any major novelist, Tolstoy's fiction is unusually autobiographical. This is no reflection upon his imagination or powers of invention, which were very considerable. But the life he transposed into art was largely his own life of recorded experience and observation, rendered infinitely effective artistically by penetrating analysis and by his subtle choice of significant psychological detail. In short, the convincing, unexaggerated realism of his fiction is rooted in autobiography. His novels seem so amazingly true to life because they are true. On the other hand, although Tolstoy is obviously drawing upon memories of his own childhood in this work, there is a great deal of sheer invention in it. For example, Nicholas remembers his mother very well and poignantly recalls his feelings at the time of her death, which is exquisitely described, but Tolstoy's mother died before he was two years old. And the gambling father of the story has nothing in common with Tolstoy's father.

There is even less of the autobiographical in the sequels— *Boyhood* (1854) and *Youth* (1857). In them, however, the poetic and evocative atmosphere of *Childhood* is not so much in evidence, and elements of intellection and psychological analysis are more dominant. Yet in these three connected short novels one savors the happy ease and self-sufficiency of large gentry families. Their intimate understanding of one another is curiously transformed into an intimate understanding between Tolstoy and the reader, a pleasurable familiarity that is carried over in his handling of the many similar families portrayed in the great novels of the future. How memorable are some of the scenes in *Childhood*, *Boyhood*, and *Youth*, in which the commonplace experiences of the young are made to seem "strange" by the witchery of art and hence endlessly attractive to the reader, such as Nicholas' thoughts when he is forced to kneel in the corner and is convinced that his tutor has forgotten him; or the youthful Irtenev who lashes his bare back with a rope in order to harden himself, and then—remembering that death may come at any moment—neglects his lessons for three days on end and lies in bed enjoying a novel and eating honey cakes which he had bought with his last remaining coins; or how Nicholas, threatened with a whipping by the hated tutor, St. Jérome, indulges in compensatory daydreaming, imagines that he has enlisted in the Hussars, is wounded, achieves glory, and then asks as his only boon from a grateful sovereign that he be allowed to kill his loathsome tutor. Finally, there are the many brilliant portraits—the kindly first tutor, Karl Ivanych, the wonderful mad man of God, Grisha, the lovable servant, Natalya Savishna, and many others. No objective detail escapes the author, and no inner meditation, however fugitive, seems beyond his grasp.

Many of the characteristic qualities of Tolstoy's mature art are already apparent in these early works. The customary initial period of imitation and immature fumbling is avoided. All the ineffable charm of childhood, boyhood, and youth is recaptured with compelling authenticity, and we live over again in these pages our own youthful joys and sorrows, dreams and hopes. With little faltering and no false moves, Tolstoy mounted at the first try the immortal steed of great art.

3

Though Tolstoy was not yet certain that he wished to settle on the career of writing, the initial success of *Childhood* encouraged him to seek new material for his pen. He found plenty of it in his Caucasian surroundings and absorbing army life; and not a few of the officers and soldiers he got to know well became the heroes and villains of his Caucasian short stories. In addition there were spectacular scenery, beautiful native girls, and the inimitable Cossack settlers in the village where his battery was stationed. Tolstoy now set out to treat realistically the themes of war and Caucasian life which only some twenty to thirty years before had been so romantically written about in exotic tales in verse and prose by his predecessors Pushkin, Marlinsky, and Lermontov.

All four of Russia's most celebrated novelists, Gogol, Dostoevsky, Turgenev, and Tolstoy, began their literary careers with the short story and each has contributed one or more tales that would find honored places in any comprehensive anthology of the country's best examples of the genre. Tolstoy continued to write short stories throughout his long life, but several of his earliest efforts are particularly important, not only for their intrinsic worth and charm, but also for an understanding of the inception and development of a narrative art which found its fullest expression in the great novels. Here we observe him eager for literary fame, agonizing over the fear of failure and then boyishly jubilant over success, yet always boldly experimenting with form and content.

Each of the Caucasian stories ("The Raid," "The Wood-Felling," and "Meeting a Moscow Acquaintance in the Detachment"), written or conceived during his two-year stay in that region, is an outgrowth of personal experience in fighting with the Russian forces against the hill tribes, or of some adventure on his furloughs. "A Billiard-Marker's Notes," despite its setting, also properly falls into the Caucasian group in the sense that it was inspired by a disastrous gambling experience Tolstoy had with a billiard-marker in Tiflis, where he had gone in 1851 to take an army examination. It is an excellent illustration of how Tolstoy can turn a rather attenuated autobiographical experience into an independent, powerful, and poignant study of moral degeneration. It is also possible that some of his own spiritual distress over loose living at this time entered into the story.

Within the limitations of the short-story form, the principal characterizations of the military figures in the Caucasian tales are studies in some depth, and the significant action is nearly always narrated with a realism quite fresh for that time. In this military environment it was almost inevitable that the youthful Tolstoy, with his restless questing mind, should reveal an interest in such abstract questions as: What constitutes bravery? ("The Raid"), or: Into what categories should soldiers be classified? ("The Wood-Felling"). Yet these concerns are never allowed to obtrude on the essential unity of the stories. And the subject that was to dominate so much of his thinking in later years—the rightness or wrongness of war—is also touched upon. In fact, in "The Raid," and to a certain extent in "The Wood-Felling," there is more than a suggestion of his later ruthless analysis of conventional thinking about military glory. But he was not yet blind to the heroism of the simple plain soldier or officer, and his accounts of incidents in this connection in "The Raid" provide the main attraction of the tale.

After more than two years in the Caucasus, Tolstoy grew weary of his life there and eventually managed to obtain a transfer to an artillery brigade in active service on the Danube, where the Russians were fighting the Turks. (He had by now obtained a commission in the army.) Not long before he left, perhaps in one of those periods of disillusion not infrequent in his youth, he wrote in his diary: "Literature is rubbish and I should like to set down here rules and a plan of estate-management." Contemporary literature was declining, he decided, because authors were producing too many light books for the sake of commercial gain. But a bit later he also noted in his diary: "Literary success that satisfies one's own self is obtained only by working at every aspect of a subject. But the subject must be a lofty one if the labor is always to be pleasant."

The trip home in January, 1854, to Yasnaya Polyana where he spent his furlough was uneventful save for a fierce blizzard that inspired his memorable story, "The Snow Storm," which was written the following year. The sole theme is the storm, but it is so vividly realized that it takes on the human attributes of an intensely imagined character. Like Chekhov's celebrated long story, *The Steppe*, which also features a storm, the tale is really a tone poem of the elements. The repeated motifs of snow and wind have almost the quality of the incremental repetition of a folk ballad. So acute is the sensuous perception of bitter cold that the reader imaginatively experiences the sensation. The striking contrast of freezing weather and the traveler's dream of a hot summer day, drawn from an incident in Tolstoy's childhood, is a most effective device.

4

Not long after Tolstoy joined the active army on the Danube in March, 1854, England and France came in on the side of the Turks and the struggle turned into the Crimean War. A wave of patriotism swept Russia when the allies besieged Sevastopol, the first invasion of the country since the time of Napoleon.

Nor was Tolstoy immune to this feeling, whatever doubts may have occurred to him about the futility of war during his Caucasian experiences. And as in the Caucasus, the muse once again vied with Mars for his devotion. He had already sent off the manuscript of *Boyhood* to the publisher, and now he continued to peck away at *The Cossacks, The Novel of a Russian Landowner,* and *Youth,* the sequel to *Boyhood.* We get a characteristic picture of the young lieutenant sitting during his off-duty hours in a bombproof shelter of the dangerously exposed Fourth Bastion of the besieged city's defenses, writing away at his first Sevastopol piece. Shells burst outside, bullets whistled over the parapet, and Tolstoy would occasionally look up from his writing to catch the macabre front-line humor of soldiers playing "Noses" or hear their quips as they entered or left the shelter.

Purists might well reject Tolstoy's three Sevastopol "sketches," as they are sometimes erroneously called, as fiction. On the other hand, one could hardly regard them as articles of a talented war correspondent. Whatever else they may be they are art of the highest quality, in the same sense that Dostoevsky's *House of the Dead* is art and not simply a reporter's write-up of his life in a Siberian prison. If these pieces are mostly accounts of what Tolstoy observed and experienced at Sevastopol, he renders them immeasurably effective by employing artistic devices of fiction—setting, careful selection of precise detail in description, dialogue, development of characters through analysis of human motivation and feelings, and in the third narrative, possibly also in the second, there is as much plot as one finds in most of his indubitable short stories.

"Sevastopol in December 1854" skilfully recaptures the spirit of the early days of the siege in a series of brilliant genre pictures of the city and swiftly limned portraits of its typical inhabitants and defenders. The chief characteristics of the strength of the Russian, Tolstoy points out in his description of the fighting men at the Fourth Bastion, are his simplicity and obstinacy. This moving but realistically frank account of the self-sacrificing heroism of the defenders and their determination to repulse the invaders raised the flagging hopes of a nation sick with the carnage and suffering of Sevastopol. A new dimension had been added to the young Tolstoy's literary popularity in Russia. A month after the publication of the piece, he entered in his diary: "Have now reached a period of real temptation through vanity. I could gain much in life if I wished to write without conviction."

"Sevastopol in May 1855," however, is emphatic proof of the firm manner in which Tolstoy turned his back on this temptation. For as the bloody siege wore on he began to understand more clearly not only the horrible futility of it, but also the base human motives and practices of men who created war and then fattened on such human folly. This altered attitude is clearly reflected in this second Sevastopol piece in ironic passages, satirical touches, and in forthright criticism of those officers whose "patriotism" is translated into terms of personal gain. Purely literary effects are not neglected, especially in the striking description of the night action. Nevertheless, Tolstoy plainly wished it to be known, as though ashamed of idealizing some aspects of war in the first Sevastopol account, that he would no longer compromise with truth, and he announced the fact in ringing terms at the end of "Sevastopol in May" in a famous sentence which may be regarded as his credo for the rest of his long life as a writer and thinker: "The hero of my tale—whom I love with all the power of my soul, whom I have tried to portray in all his beauty, who has been, is, and will be beautiful—is Truth."

In a letter to Nekrasov, editor of the *Contemporary*, which accompanied the manuscript of the second Sevastopol piece, Tolstoy wrote: "Although I'm convinced that it is incomparably better than the first, I'm certain that it will not be liked."

This was an understatement. The angry chairman of the Censor's Commission denounced the manuscript because of its "ridicule of our brave officers, the brave defenders of Sevastopol." He agreed to its printing only after he had entirely altered the tone of the narrative by changes and deletions. Then, when the editor refused to publish it, the censor insisted, for he realized that he had virtually transformed the piece into a propaganda document for the government. The editor, however, would not place Tolstoy's name on "Sevastopol in May" when it appeared in print.

The chagrined Nekrasov wrote Tolstoy of his indignation over what had happened: "Your work, of course, will not be lost . . . it will always remain as proof of a strength that was able to speak such profound and sober truth in circumstances amid which few men would have retained it. . . . You are right to value that side of your gifts most of all. Truth—in the form you have introduced it into our literature—is something entirely new among us. I do not know another writer of today who so compels the reader to love him and sympathize heartily with him as he to whom I now write. And I only fear lest time, the nastiness of life, and the deafness and dumbness that surround us, should do to you what it has done to most of us, and kill the energy without which there can be no writer—none at least such as Russia needs."

Sevastopol was abandoned by the Russians in August, 1855, and Tolstoy was happy to be sent as a courier to Petersburg in November. It was there, in the course of the next month, that he wrote "Sevastopol in August 1855." Now, in this third narrative, on the fall of the besieged city, he is very much the storyteller. Well-developed characters, especially the Kozeltsov brothers, add an increment of unity to a loosely constructed plot. In the studied objectivity, and particularly in the leisurely, panoramic method of narration, and in the manner in which plot is sacrificed to accumulating detail, one may detect the influence of Thackeray, whom the young Tolstoy had been eagerly reading and admiring over this period. Though the lyric passages of the first Sevastopol piece are not duplicated, some of the didacticism of the second is present in the arraignment of peculation in commissary matters, a practice that deeply troubled Tolstoy and one which, when he refused to subscribe to it, got him into serious difficulties with his fellow officers. But the whole narrative is suffused with a tragic note of despair over the abandonment of the city where so many thousands had perished and which heroic soldiers were still ready to defend. The treatment of war and the characterizations of military figures in the three Sevastopol pieces anticipate Tolstoy's artistic achievements in these respects in *War and Peace*.

5

Back in Petersburg, Tolstoy, now sick of war, sent in his resignation from the army. While waiting for an official acceptance, he enjoyed the social life of the capital and his reputation as a literary hero established by the popularity of the Sevastopol pieces. Under the eager sponsorship of the older Turgenev, Petersburg's literary leader at that time, the twenty-seven-year-old Tolstoy was soon presented to many important authors, and publishers and magazine editors competed for his writings. The liberal wing of the progressive *Contemporary*, which he had previously favored, sought his support against the emerging radical group connected with this important magazine. But Tolstoy preferred to do his own thinking and was a bit contemptuous of principles or opinions which he himself had not advanced. Turgenev's letter to P. A. Annenkov hits off the curious prickly charm of the young literary hero: "Imagine, for more than two weeks now Tolstoy has been living with me, and what I would not give to see you both together! You cannot picture to yourself what a dear and remarkable man he is, although I have nicknamed him the 'troglodyte,' because of his savage ardor and buffalo-like obstinacy." Tolstoy disliked the radicals of the *Contemporary* and condemned the liberals for what he thought was the insincerity of men who failed to practice what they preached. He soon quarrelled with Turgenev and ended by offending the leadership of the *Contemporary*, whose growing emphasis upon social significance in literature disturbed him.

During 1856 Tolstoy continued his literary efforts, publishing two short stories already mentioned, "Meeting a Moscow Acquaintance in the Detachment" and "The Snow Storm," a large fragment of a novel, *A Landlord's Morning*, and the fine short novel, *Two Hussars*. He also made much progress on longer works, especially *Youth*, which was published the next year, and in 1856 his first collection, *Army Tales*, appeared, and *Childhood* and *Boyhood* in a single edition. Now for the first time, however, critical reaction to his fiction was cool, even hostile, perhaps a reflection of the changing attitude of liberal Petersburg critics whom he had annoyed and who found in these tales no political or social significance that would respond to the progressive spirit of the age. Meanwhile Tolstoy was evincing a desire to strike out on new literary paths far removed from the popular demand. He entered in his diary: "How I long to have done with magazines in order to write in the way I'm now beginning to think about art: awfully lofty and pure."

At the end of 1856 Tolstoy at last received his discharge from the army and in January of the next year he set out on his first trip to Western Europe, a journey that he had long been anticipating. All the excitement of touring in strange countries absorbed his intense nature and left little time for developing his thoughts about the new direction which his literary art must take. Then, before a fashionable hotel at Lucerne, occurred the incident of the little itinerant singer whose songs

the wealthy tourists appreciated but absent-mindedly neglected to reward. In a very short time the outraged Tolstoy
dashed off that powerful homily in fiction—"Lucerne." It is
hardly an example of the new art he was thinking about, but it
does mark a significant shift of focus from the objective realism of his war tales to what might be described as subjective
realism with a moralistic emphasis. Here he deliberately employs his art to illuminate and condemn the materialistic civilization of the West by comparing the shallowness and human
insensitivity of its sophisticated members with the natural man
represented by the little street singer. In this fictionalized moralistic tract the voice of Rousseau rings loud and clear in
Tolstoy's effort to oppose nature, morality, and art to political
laws and organized government. "Lucerne" is a signpost pointing the direction of much of his future thought.

Although "Albert," which was also written abroad, may
have been an effort along the lines of the "awfully lofty and
pure" art which Tolstoy had mentioned in his diary, it is
infected, in a negative sense, with the moralizing of "Lucerne."
In any event, he was concerned with the question of art which
he firmly believed must be based upon moral truths that went
deeper than the "convictions" of the politically and socially
minded contributors to the *Contemporary*, and "Albert" was
intended to convey this belief. For the story, which may have
been connected with Tolstoy's experiences with a talented but
drunken violinist whom he had befriended, is essentially a
protest against society's inability to understand and protect real
art. The trouble is that the morally sick musician seems more in
need of a doctor than the encouragement of a heedless public
incapable of appreciating virtuoso performances on the violin.
The tale is saved, however, by the fine lyrical description of
the effect of superb music on a listener, a scene obviously
inspired by Tolstoy's own powerful reaction to music.

In the case of the brief story "Three Deaths" there can be no doubt that Tolstoy wrote it to exemplify the moral truth of pure art. Without questioning the very concept of pure art, critics have differed on the effectiveness of its realization in this tale. In any event, the moral truth brought out in the contrast between harmony with creation in the death of the old peasant and the tree and disharmony in the death of the querulous invalid lady is altogether too pat and artistically unadorned to carry conviction.

When Tolstoy returned to Russia from abroad in the middle of 1857, he was chagrined to discover that his literary reputation had vanished. "Lucerne" and "Albert" puzzled both public and critics and, later, "Three Deaths" did not help the situation. It was whispered about that he had lost his grip, that the great literary promise of his early fiction had come to nought. And in the light of the social tendentiousness that now gripped literature, it was not surprising that in his next considerable effort, *Family Happiness* (1859), a short novel inspired by an early love affair, he should once again disappoint readers and critics.

Perhaps a feeling that he was out of tune with contemporary demands in literature, in addition to an urge he had experienced abroad to find new outlets for his incredible energies, prompted Tolstoy to give up creative writing at this time and plunge into the exciting field of educational theory and practice. Over the next three years he ran his fascinating school for peasant children at Yasnaya Polyana and wrote extensively on educational matters.

Marriage in 1862 to Sophia Bers brought to an end Tolstoy's educational experiments and reawakened in him the urge to resume his creative writing. He completed a brilliant story of peasant life, *Polikushka*, and *The Cossacks*, an outstanding short novel, both of which were published in 1863. And that same year he wrote a short tale, "Strider: The Story of a Horse," which did not appear in print until years later. The idea for it may have been suggested by an incident that took place in 1856, when Tolstoy visited Turgenev's estate. On one of their walks together the two writers passed before an old broken-down horse and Tolstoy, patting it affectionately, began to describe what he imagined the horse was thinking and feeling at that moment. The account was so vivid that the astonished and delighted host declared that Tolstoy must at one time have been a horse. In any event, his equine hero is modeled on a real horse, Kholstomer, quite celebrated in Russia for his enormous stride and speed. Tolstoy may have refused to publish the story at this time because it could easily have been construed as a contribution to the literature of social significance which he so much deplored. For the tale is really a satire, from the point of view of a horse, against the evils of modern society, especially the institution of property. The uncanny manner in which Tolstoy humanizes the horse by projecting himself into the consciousness of the poor old piebald gelding is remarkable and an artistic *tour de force*. In the end, after the sustained realism of the animal's horrible death, the horse emerges as a more useful and dignified creature than its human owners.

The curious little story, "The Porcelain Doll," was Tolstoy's share of a joint letter which he and his pregnant wife wrote to her sister in 1863. On the surface it appears to be a slight thing intended merely to amuse both his wife and his sister-in-law, but throughout this deftly turned miniature tale there are repeated hints of marital discontent. Tolstoy, a tremendously active and passionate man, deeply resented the frigidity of his young wife, particularly accentuated during her first pregnancy. She noted in her diary at this time: "The role of the physical side of love plays a great part in him. And that is awful. For me, on the contrary, it means nothing." The porcelain doll of the story is a symbol of his intense emotional frustration. However, his naïve wife seems to have missed the point, for at the end of the letter she comments to her sister: "He has invented this that I am porcelain, such a rascal! But what does it mean—God knows."

This revival of interest in creative writing at the time of his marriage supports the conviction that Tolstoy could no more give up literature than he could cease his search for truth; one was the essential medium for the expression of the other. At the low point of the chilly reaction of the critics to his fictional efforts in 1859, Tolstoy delivered an unusual address to the Moscow Society of Lovers of Russian Literature. He deplored the fact that the public and the critics had begun to think that the problem of all literature consists only in the denunciation of evil, in the debate and correction of it, in short, in the growth of a civic feeling in society. On the contrary, he concluded his remarks: "There is another literature, reflecting eternal and universal human interests, the most precious, sincere consciousness of the people, a literature accessible to every people and to all times, a literature without which no single people, gifted with strength and richness, has ever developed."

An important step toward the creation of such a literature in Russia had been the fiction so far commented upon in this first period, to which must also be added a series of early short novels.

I I

EARLY SHORT NOVELS

I

During Tolstoy's first literary period, before he embarked on *War and Peace*, he experimented with a fictional form longer than the short story yet considerably shorter than a full-length novel. The Russians have a felicitous word for this genre, *povest*, which is defined in their dictionaries as: "A literary work of a narrative nature, in size less than a novel." We employ several designations for it: "long short story," "novelette," "short novel," and, quite improperly, "novella." With some arbitrariness I have chosen the term "short novel" for such works, for it seems most adequately to suggest their form and content as well as the fact that in these tales Tolstoy was consciously preparing himself to undertake the full-length novel.

Two Hussars, A Landlord's Morning, Family Happiness, Polikushka, and *The Cossacks* are Tolstoy's only short novels during these early years, with the possible exception of *Childhood, Boyhood,* and *Youth.* The latter three, however, are interrelated narratives and, taken together—the form in which they are so frequently published—must be regarded as a full-length novel. These five short novels, in addition to the seventeen pieces already discussed in the preceding chapter, constitute all the completed fiction that Tolstoy wrote between 1851 and 1863, his first literary period.

Though Tolstoy excelled in the short-story form from the beginning of his writing career, its artistic restrictions were alien to the natural bent of his expansive genius. Hence his early efforts in the short novel, often brilliantly realized, represent a transition to the more artistically congenial, spacious, and complex world of *War and Peace* and *Anna Karenina*. Specifically, he began to reveal more care for settings, greater psychological density, and the ability to cope with a larger number of characters in intricate human relations.

In *Two Hussars* (1856), the earliest of this group of short novels and Tolstoy's first piece of fiction based on a theme outside his personal experience, one is immediately aware, in comparison with his previous writing, of maturing artistic powers. The juxtaposition of two generations reflecting alternating contrasts in the personalities and adventures of father and son became a favorite fictional device which Tolstoy later used in his long novels on a much more elaborate scale. Count Fyodor Turbin, a handsome, fire-eating young hussar, appears for one night in a provincial town and throws its society into turmoil by his fearlessness, drinking, and wild escapades, and before departing he seduces a pretty young widow. Yet no one is shocked by his behavior, for his daring, generosity, and noble nature win the admiration of all.

Twenty years later another young hussar officer, the son of Count Fyodor Turbin, who has been killed in a duel, arrives with his troops in the same provincial town. By chance he is quartered in the widow's house and unsuccessfully attempts to seduce her pretty daughter. The son, a calculating, materialistic prig, is entirely unlike his lovable scapegrace of a father.

The contrast between them, as well as between the two generations they represent, is deliberate. In the son, Tolstoy is condemning his own generation in favor of an older one for which he had a familiar nostalgic hankering. But in so doing, the portrayal of the son is much less convincing than that of his father, an artistic fault which Tolstoy seemed to recognize. For in his diary he noted a friend's remark that the son is described without love, and he commented in his notebook at this time: "The first condition of an author's popularity, that is, the way to make himself loved, is the love with which he treats all his characters." It was a mistake he rarely made later. He learned, in observing the human condition, that man does not go through the wringer of life and emerge all white. "Every man," he declared in *Resurrection*, "carries in himself the germ of every human quality, but sometimes it is one quality that manifests itself and sometimes another."

Actually, Tolstoy was greatly attracted, in real life as well as in fiction, to strong, bold, intense personalities like that of the father in *Two Hussars* or Eroshka in *The Cossacks*, and he willingly forgives their violent actions and moral lapses when committed out of an excess of their passionate nature. Some of the scenes in *Two Hussars* are extremely well handled, such as the party at the gypsies and the poetic dreams of the widow's charming daughter Lisa as she stands at the window in the moonlight, an early preview of the famous scene of Natasha in *War and Peace* when she contemplates from her bedroom window the moonlit beauty of a perfect spring night.

2

In *A Landlord's Morning* and *Polikushka*, Tolstoy for the first time is mainly concerned with peasants, a class that played a role, but not a dominant one, in his later fiction. And in *A Landlord's Morning* (1856) he also returns to events of his personal life, which had furnished themes for so many of his early tales. His initial intention, which he abandoned, was to write a full-length novel about a landowner's experiences with his peasants, and the present short novel appears to be the self-contained opening section of this project. At the beginning of it, the nineteen-year-old Nekhlyudov writes his aunt that he has given up his studies at the university in order to devote himself to the affairs of his estate and especially to trying to remedy the pitiable and impoverished conditions of his hundreds of peasants. He explains, in a spirit of high idealism, that it is his sacred duty to care for their welfare, and that to guide his endeavors he has written down rules of conduct for himself.

At the age of nineteen, Tolstoy also left the university to live on his estate, Yasnaya Polyana, in order to fulfil a new humanitarian "purpose in life"—to improve the lot of his many serfs, over whom he was then absolute master. And he too, like Nekhlyudov, wrote out rules of conduct. In doing good for the peasantry he was convinced that he would find real happiness.

Unfortunately, we have no definite information about Tolstoy's activities in this first attempt to reform his fellow men. Several years later a diary note on the plan of the proposed novel suggests what his intentions had been in this experiment, and the consequences that followed: "The hero searches for the realization of an ideal of happiness and justice in a country existence. Not finding it, he becomes disillusioned and wishes to search for his ideal in family life. His friend introduces him to the thought that happiness does not consist of an ideal but may be found in continued vital work that has for its purpose the happiness of others."

It may be assumed that Tolstoy's course of action paralleled that of his hero in *A Landlord's Morning*. Nekhlyudov, who refuses to regard the poverty of his peasants as an unavoidable evil, abolishes corporal punishment and provides schooling and medical aid for them. Like a ministering angel, he visits their wretched, filthy hovels, described by Tolstoy with that saturation of precise detail which became a hallmark of his realism. In simple-hearted fashion, Nekhlyudov pours out his willingness to devote his life to their happiness. But his first fine rapture does not last long. Despite all his efforts, the peasants remain poor, shirk education, and do not improve morally. Somehow his plans all come to nothing. The peasants are endlessly suspicious and regard his offers of aid as just another trick on the part of the master to get more work out of them. Perplexed in the extreme and sadly disillusioned, he finally abandons his experiment.

If the young Tolstoy's similar efforts at Yasnaya Polyana were equally feckless, he was probably not above subjecting his motives to the kind of acute self-criticism which we find in the tale in the response of Nekhlyudov's aunt to her nephew's undertaking. One does not believe in arguments and rules but only in experience, she writes, and experience tells her that his plans are childish. "You always wished to appear original," she declares, "but your originality is really nothing but excessive self-esteem."

Turgenev, in a letter to a friend, argues that *A Landlord's Morning* conveys the unpleasant impression that all efforts of landowners to improve conditions of the peasantry lead to nothing. The real moral of the work, however, is that so long as serfdom exists the master will be unable to better the lot of his peasants, despite disinterested endeavors to do so. Tolstoy clearly recognized this fact, and one may perceive a connection between *A Landlord's Morning* and his attempt, in the course of the year it was published (1856), to free his own serfs. But they rejected the offer, which was carefully contrived to protect his interests in the land, perhaps because he once again failed to take into consideration the innate hostility for the master that centuries of serfdom had implanted in the peasantry. Rather bitterly he commented in his diary: "Two powerful men are joined with a sharp chain; it hurts both of them, and when one of them moves, he involuntarily cuts the other, and neither has room to work." *A Landlord's Morning* gives effective artistic expression to this profound antagonism and at the same time illuminates with striking clarity the nature of the Russian peasant and the unbelievably shocking conditions under which he lived.

Though *Polikushka* (1863) was published after the emancipation of the serfs in 1861, it is concerned, like *A Landlord's Morning*, with peasant existence before they obtained their freedom. But here the emphasis is quite different. There is no autobiographical element, no personal thesis to develop. Tolstoy's concentration is entirely upon telling a gripping story of peasant life, and he does it with infinite art. The result is a masterpiece in the genre of the short novel.

Tolstoy's maturing artistic powers are much in evidence in this tale. The wretched peasant Polikushka, who drinks too much, is a liar, and finds it hard to keep his "pickers and feelers" off the loose property of anyone, joyfully dreams of justifying his mistress' faith in him by safely fulfilling her commission to bring the package of money from town. His terrible despair over the collapse of his hopes because of the accidental loss of the money on the way home is compounded by the realization that no one will ever believe him if he tells the truth. To kill himself seems the only way out of his impossible dilemma.

Tolstoy adds convincingness to this tragic incident by placing it in a setting of remarkably described peasant existence: the subtly handled relations of the mistress of the estate to her steward and his to the peasants of the village; the superb picture of the superstitious terror of these simple people over Polikushka's suicide; old Dutlov's similar fear that the found money, which had been given to him by his mistress, is the evil

money of the devil; and the splendid, almost Dostoevskian
scene in the tavern where old Dutlov, who uses the "evil
money" to buy up a substitute for his nephew conscripted
into the army, bows down before the "hired" recruit, who has
offended him, and asks his forgiveness.

Though Tolstoy's superb sense of reality often leads him to
indicate a disillusioning truth or at least a disappointing truth,
in this superbly ironic ending he avoids the position of the
habitual cynic who can be as false to reality as the habitual
idealist. If Dutlov had lost his mistress' money and Polikushka
had found it, he would most likely have squandered it. The
cynical writer might well have had Dutlov do the same, but
instead he uses it for a worthy purpose—to save his son from
the army in order that the young man might aid his needy
family. The irony cuts deep here and simply because Tolstoy's
understanding of reality is so just.

No wonder that Turgenev, who at this time had little reason
to be well disposed toward his irascible friend Tolstoy, wrote
the poet Fet that after reading *Polikushka* he "marvelled at the
strength of his [Tolstoy's] huge talent. But he has used up too
much material, and it is a pity he drowned the son. It makes it
too terrible. But there are pages that are truly wonderful. It
makes a cold shudder run down even my back, and you know
my back has grown thick and course. He is a master, a master!"

Tolstoy had indeed become a master. Without being tendentious, *Polikushka* exposes the hard features of peasant life. The
tone of refined humor that aimed to ridicule the false and
insincere in art appeared for the first time in his fiction. On this
same high level of performance, he continued to write about
the peasant and his relation to the landowner in brilliant sections of *War and Peace* and *Anna Karenina.*

Family Happiness (1859) is a most interesting example of
the manner in which Tolstoy transposes the facts of real life
into the substance of art. It will be remembered that in his plan

for a novel about a Russian landowner, of which *A Landlord's Morning* is all he completed, the hero, after his disillusionment in reforming his peasants, seeks a new ideal in family life. Tolstoy himself long pursued this ideal of family happiness, and during 1856–57 he actively sought the realization of it in courting pretty Valerya Arseneva, much younger than himself, who lived on an estate not far from Yasnaya Polyana. Somewhat like Sergei Mihkailych in *Family Happiness*, Tolstoy had easy access to the young lady's house as the guardian of her brother. And again like the hero of the short novel, he employed an imaginary second-self to explain his feelings to Valerya, urged her to practice his favorite piano pieces, and grew wrathy over her fondness for high society.

Although Tolstoy allowed himself to become deeply committed to Valerya, in the end, unlike Sergei Mikhailych in the story, he shrank from marriage with her because he lost faith in it as an ideal of happiness. "I never loved her with real love," he wrote a family friend. "I was carried away by the reprehensible desire to inspire love. This gave me a delight I had never before experienced. . . . I have behaved very badly."

No doubt a felt need to justify his shabby conduct and purge his mind of the whole episode drove Tolstoy to write *Family Happiness*, in which he tries to indicate that if he and Valerya had married, their different views of what made for happiness in such a relationship would have led to unhappiness for both. But he transforms the experience of real life, in the first part of the tale, into a charming, poetic narrative of the dawning love of a sensitive seventeen-year-old girl for a man twice her age, a contemporary of her father, and also her guardian. All we know of Tolstoy's relationship with Valerya comes from his letters and diary entries. In his short novel the challenge of art compels Tolstoy to tell the story of the love of Masha and her guardian as it is seen through the eyes of this young girl. It is a delicate psychological study in depth, a

worthy forerunner of the moving love stories of his great
novels. We observe how the mysterious chemistry of love
gradually and insensibly alters the nature of the youthful,
inexperienced Masha and reveals to her "a whole new world of
joys in the present, without changing anything in my life,
without adding anything except himself to each impression of
my mind. All that had surrounded me from childhood without
saying anything to me suddenly came to life. The mere sight
of him made everything begin to speak and press for admit-
tance to my heart, filling it with happiness."

Yet it is interesting to see how Tolstoy, as always, qualifies
the idealizing poetry of his heroine by the sober truth of fact.
A few days before her marriage Masha takes the sacrament,
and her thoughts are suffused by the elation of lofty religious
feelings. She ecstatically wonders how much more they will be
elated by actual marriage with the man she loves. However,
after the ceremony is performed she is described as "only
frightened and disappointed: all was over but nothing extraordinary, nothing worthy of the sacrament I had received had
taken place in myself."

The radiant poetic atmosphere of the first part of the story is
dissipated in the second part by the familiar stresses and strains
of married life. Masha eventually grows impatient with the
uneventfulness of country existence with her husband and
craves the movement and excitement of high society in the
city. Although he has lived this kind of social life himself and is
aware of its shallowness, he bows to the wishes of his young
wife. Her social success and eager willingness to sacrifice to it
the values he prized most in her soon bring about an estrange-
ment in their relations. At this point Tolstoy may be accused
of introducing into his story a didactic puritanical element.
Quite clearly he wished to suggest that the disparity in years,
experience, and tastes inevitably erode the family happiness of
Masha and her husband, just as they would have done if he had

married Valerya. The conclusion of the story, however, saves the situation by a solution that does not appear to be false either to the reality of things or to the demands of art. Tormented by the conviction that she has lost his love, Masha at last confronts her husband with an anguished plea for an explanation. They sit on the veranda of her old house, and here the reluctant husband, prompted by tender memories of their first ecstasies and the antiphonal responses of nature as gentle summer rain clouds shadow the setting sun, offers a clarification. She accuses him of not continuing to love her as at the beginning of their marriage and of failing to exercise his authority and greater experience to save her from the mistakes she made in pursuing the illusion of social success. She had to learn this by her own experience, he tells her, and if their early passionate love has vanished, this was inevitable anyway. It can now be replaced, he adds, by another kind of love, a peaceful love. "Don't let us try to repeat life," he declares. "Don't let us make pretences to ourselves. Let us be thankful that there is an end of the old emotions and excitements. The excitement of searching is over for us; our quest is done, and happiness enough has fallen to our lot. Now we must stand aside and make room for him," he concludes, pointing to their infant son whom the nurse was carrying out to the veranda for their nightly blessing.

3

The Cossacks (1863), the last and longest of the pieces in this group was planned as the first part of a three-part novel which Tolstoy never completed, but the work as it stands has a beginning, middle, and end, and the inner unity of a well-rounded short novel. He began it in 1852 during his stay in the Caucasus as a cadet in the Russian army, but because of many interruptions he did not finish it until ten years later, shortly after his marriage in 1862. In fact, if he had not felt obliged to the publisher of it for an advance of a thousand roubles to pay off a gambling debt, it is possible that he might never have completed *The Cossacks*.

As the subtitle, "A Tale of 1852," indicates, the story concerns events of that year. At that time, when not off on a campaign, Tolstoy was quartered in the Grebensk Cossack village of Starogladkov and lived more or less the life vividly described in *The Cossacks*. Though it is unwise to push autobiographical correspondences too far, certain obvious sources are worth pointing out. Tolstoy stayed in the house of the old Cossack, Epishka Sekhin, who is quite faithfully portrayed as the remarkable Daddy Eroshka in the tale. And in her way, the equally impressive Maryanka was modeled on the beautiful Starogladkov Cossack girl Solomonida, as impervious to Tolstoy's attentions as the heroine is to Olenin's. Both girls preferred a dashing young Cossack like Lukashka in the story, who killed Chechens, stole horses, got drunk, and at night climbed in the window of his sweetheart without thinking who he was or why he existed.

The ambivalence of Olenin, a struggle in him between the social and moral claims of the cultured society into which he had been born and the simple, amoral way of life of these Cossack children of nature, reflects in part Tolstoy's struggle during his more than two years of service in the Caucasus. Under the influence of his new surroundings, Olenin learns to condemn artificial civilization, yet he finds it difficult to accept wholeheartedly the views of Daddy Eroshka, who thinks all religion is a fraud and declares: "God has made everything for the joy of man. There is no sin in any of it." But Olenin definitely regards it as a sin when this old reprobate offers to provide a beauty for him. "A sin?" he shouts. "Where's the sin? A sin to look at a nice girl? A sin to have some fun with her? Or is it a sin to love her? Is that so in your parts? . . . No, my dear fellow, it's not a sin, it's salvation! God made you and

God made the girl too. He made it all; so it is no sin to look at a nice girl. That's what she was made for: to be loved and to give joy."

The natural beauty of Cossack existence transforms Olenin into a philosophical reasoner searching for personal happiness, a kind of Rousseauistic "natural man," a type that became a favorite of Tolstoy in later fiction. Under the impact of these people, unspoiled by civilization, Olenin envisages his personal pursuit of happiness in terms of self-sacrifice and love for others. But this romantic ideal is shattered by his passionate love for Maryanka, who is utterly inaccessible to him as a non-Cossack incapable of ever identifying himself with their emancipated life.

The Cossacks is the final work of Tolstoy's first literary period, and no doubt it is his finest during these twelve years. Turgenev did not hesitate to pronounce it "the best story that has been written in our language." Though there are artistic flaws in the portrait of Olenin, the principal Cossack characters, Eroshka, Lukashka, and Maryanka, are among the most memorable of Tolstoy's creations. With them, one experiences that baffling impression, which is the quintessence of his realism, that somehow these characters are telling their own stories without the author's intervention beyond that of acting as an occasional commentator. And that inner truth of a work of fiction, which must come from life itself, seems more fully developed in *The Cossacks* than in any other tale of Tolstoy's first literary period.

The work helped to win back some of Tolstoy's popularity with the reading public, but the radical-democratic critics, sensing the implied condemnation of all modern society in *The Cossacks*, gave it only grudging praise. It is true that a number of the characters in Tolstoy's early tales come close to being merely emanations of himself, and only the best of them are psychologically alive. But whether he is treating war, family

happiness, or exemplifying moral truths, in both subject matter
and in his method of conquering reality by a fresh, uninhibited
analysis of human thought and action, Tolstoy was moving
artistically in the direction of the famous novels to come. He
was ready, in 1863, for the long hard task that led to his
greatest contribution to Russian literature—*War and Peace*.

III

WRITINGS
ON EDUCATION

At the end of Tolstoy's first literary period, before his marriage and the beginning of *War and Peace*, disillusionment with literature and art turned his thoughts to problems of education. A series of experiments resulted in a collection of educational writings that are both fascinating and important and all too frequently overlooked by students of Tolstoy. These publications, apart from their intrinsic value to progressive educational thinking, clearly anticipate in intellectual quality and style the much larger body of religious and philosophical works after his spiritual revelation, and they also have a real connection with later theorizing in his notable treatise, *What Is Art?*

After Tolstoy's speech at the Moscow Society of Lovers of Russian Literature in 1859, the president of that organization, devoted to popular views of the immediate social significance of literature, coldly reminded him that, however eternal truth and beauty may be in art, the artist is a man of his own times, and that the present historical moment was one in which self-indictment acquired a special meaning and an indefeasible right and hence must manifest itself in literature.

The time would come when Tolstoy's own views on literature for the people would radically change, but at the moment he had reached a point of despair and thought of abandoning literature forever. To scribble stories was stupid and shameful, he told A. A. Fet in a burst of enthusiastic confidence when he learned that this poet was thinking of settling on an estate near him and subordinating literature to farming. Literary friends, learning of his intention to plunge into educational theory and start a school at Yasnaya Polyana, pleaded with him not to deprive Russia of his literary leadership. He answered that his new endeavors bore a direct connection with his retreat from literature. For whom did Russian authors write, he asked? For themselves and the cultured few. For masses of illiterate Russian peasants literature was useless. If they could not read his writings, then he would teach them. This, he declared, was the first and essential step toward the creation of a "literature for the people." Here was a purpose that would satisfy his thirst for activity and moral influence.

When Tolstoy opened his school in the autumn of 1859 in a single room of his large manor house at Yasnaya Polyana, free education for peasant children did not exist in Russia. Occasionally, a village would boast of a priest or an ex-soldier who taught a few children at so much per head. The subjects were elementary, the method a mixture of blows and learning by heart, and the results negligible. This situation Tolstoy wished to remedy by substituting public education based on entirely original pedagogical methods.

With half a year of highly successful teaching behind him, it was almost inevitable that Tolstoy should find himself bedeviled in a maze of speculation on pedagogy and obsessed with schemes for improving national education. In March, 1860, he wrote to a friend, E. P. Kovalevsky, brother of the Minister of National Education, of his efforts and mentioned that he already had fifty students and that the number was growing. "Wisdom in all worldly affairs it seems to me," he continued, "consists not in recognizing what must be done but in knowing what to do first and then what comes after." He boldly questioned the value to progress in Russia of roads, the telegraph, literature, and the arts, as long as only about one per cent of some seventy millions of people were literate. As a remedy he proposed the establishment of a Society of National Education. Among its duties would be setting up public schools where they were most needed, designing courses of instruction, training teachers in suitable educational methods, and publishing a journal devoted to the dissemination of the society's pedagogical ideals.

Tolstoy received no official encouragement for his proposed program, but from the evidence of fragments of pedagogical essays at this time it is obvious that he had begun to think out his own course of instruction. In one fragment, entitled "On the Problems of Pedagogy," he wrote: "For every living condition of development, there is a pedagogical expediency, and to search this out is the problem of pedagogy."

Aware that he was trying, without sufficient knowledge, to handle large abstract concepts of educational theory, which in Russia were entirely dominated by Western European influence, he went abroad in 1860 to study them at the source. A full account of this effort reveals how thoroughly he pursued his objective. He visited schools and participated in classroom work in Germany, France, and England; he talked with teachers and leading educational theorists in these countries; and he collected and studied quantities of textbook samples and read numerous foreign treatises on education. After visiting schools at Kissingen, he jotted down in his diary: "It is terrible! Prayers for the king; blows; everything by rote; terrified, beaten children." Another entry shortly after: "The idea of experimental pedagogy agitates me. I can scarcely contain myself. . . ." And in still a third entry, after reading Montaigne, he wrote: "In education, once more, the chief things are equality and freedom."

Julius Froebel, nephew of Friedrich Froebel the celebrated educational reformer and founder of the kindergarten system, has left an interesting account of his discussion with Tolstoy: " 'Progress in Russia,' he told me, 'must come out of public education, which among us will give better results than in Germany, because the Russian masses are not yet spoiled by false education.' " Tolstoy went on to inform him of his own school in which learning was in no sense obligatory. " 'If education is good,' he said, 'then the need for it will manifest itself like hunger.' " And Froebel also relates that Tolstoy spoke of the Russian masses as a "mysterious and irrational force," from which one day would emerge an entirely new organization of the world, and said that from the Russian artel would develop in the future a communistic structure.

This report reflects the proud, dogmatic, almost arrogant attitude that Tolstoy adopted toward European personalities he met on this educational study trip. While sincerely seeking knowledge, he invariably made it clear that he belonged to no school of thought, had his own point of view on most questions, and that Europeans did not understand the real failings of their civilization.

From his visits to the schools of Marseille, Tolstoy took away a gloomy impression of the futility of the subjects taught and the lifeless, unimaginative methods of teaching them. On the other hand, when he talked with workers and children on the streets, he found them intelligent, free-thinking, and surprisingly well informed, but with no thanks to their schooling.

This situation led him to conclude in a later account of these experiences, in an article entitled "On National Education": "Here is an unconscious school undermining a compulsory school and making its contents almost of no worth. . . . What I saw in Marseille and in all other countries amounts to this: everywhere the principal part in educating a people is played not by schools, but by life." This is the kind of characteristic half-truth that Tolstoy was fond of deducing from incomplete experience, and it became an important factor in his educational theorizing. But even half-truths that blasted away the hard shell of traditional and erroneous thinking on vital social problems had their value for him.

2

Tolstoy returned to Russia in the spring of 1861. He erected a three-room schoolhouse at Yasnaya Polyana, and, with several teachers employed to assist him in the instruction, he worked for the next year and a half with self-sacrificing zeal on theoretical and practical problems of education. He expounded his theories and described his practice in twelve extensive articles and a series of notes published in a magazine he founded called *Yasnaya Polyana*, the issues of which appeared between February, 1862, and March, 1863. Teachers and students also contributed to the magazine. Much of what follows here is based upon Tolstoy's articles, which for that time were quite original in substance but often weakened by perverse and exasperatingly dogmatic reasoning. Though truth was his sole aim, he occasionally forgot that his sweeping generalizations were based on limited experience with his own little school and on the efforts of unique students and a unique teacher. A persistent skepticism was the trade secret of his thinking in educational matters as in other fields of human endeavor.

Over the door of the school Tolstoy placed the inscription: "Enter and Leave Freely." Perhaps he was thinking, by way of contrast, of Dante's inscription over hell: "Abandon Hope, All Ye who Enter Here," which he would hardly have hesitated to place above the entrance to most European schools he had visited. Certainly the atmosphere of his own school convinced the children that education was a precious and joyous heritage.

Tolstoy believed that all education should be free and voluntary. He supported the desire of the masses for education, but he denied that the government or any other authority had the right to force it upon them. The logic of things, and his study of the operation of compulsory education abroad, convinced him that in this form it was an evil. Pupils should come to learn of their own accord, for if education were a good, it would be found as necessary as the air they breathed. If people were antagonistic, then the will of the people should become the guiding factor. Tolstoy's faith in the "will of the people," even though the people might oppose commonly accepted notions of progress, contained the seeds of his later anarchism, and was a direct slap at radical reformers who would uplift the masses against their will.

Tolstoy also believed that education should answer the needs of the masses, but his conception of their needs had nothing in common with that of contemporary progressive thinkers. Nor did he have any patience with the widespread pedagogical conviction that education should mold the character and improve the morals of students. These were matters for family influence, he declared, and the teacher had no right to introduce his personal moral standards or social convictions into the sanctity of the home. In public education he was concerned primarily with peasants, the vast majority of the population. But he was not bent on elevating them above their class by the power of education (a definite evil in his eyes); he was concerned with making them better, more successful, and happier peasants.

In this context the individualistic direction of Tolstoy's

thought was apparent. The assumption of civilization's progress in Macaulay, Buckle, and especially in Hegel, he firmly rejected. For some time opposition between the good of the individual and the good of society had been troubling him. He was already developing a philosophy hostile to the pragmatic ideal that progress could be achieved only by social education of the people through the medium of democracy. Progress was personal, he felt, and not social. Education must serve the individual and not society, for the individual's capacity to serve humanity was what gave meaning to life. Yet he did not appear to see the contradiction in his rejection of the whole modern concept of progress. He would teach the peasant child what he needed, but what he needed was often conditioned by the social system in which he lived.

In his article "On National Education" Tolstoy defined education as "a human activity based on desire for equality and a constant tendency or urge to advance in knowledge." Education, he asserted, was history and therefore had no final aim. Its only method was experience; its only criterion, freedom.

3

Tolstoy attempted to realize in practice even the more extreme aspects of his educational philosophy. Since he believed that the functioning of a school must be adapted to the peculiar conditions of the pupils, he conceded that his own village school might well be the worst possible model for those elsewhere. Attendance was non-compulsory and free to all. Classes ordinarily ran from eight o'clock to noon and then from three o'clock to six, but, as Tolstoy proudly wrote a friend, the students often continued an hour or more beyond closing time, "because it is impossible to send the children away—they beg for more."

During the morning, elementary and advanced reading were taught, composition, penmanship, grammar, sacred history,

Russian history, drawing, music, mathematics, natural sciences, and religion; in the afternoon there were experiments in physical sciences and lessons in singing, reading, and composition. No consistent order was followed, however, and lessons were lengthened or omitted according to the degree of interest manifested by the students. On Sundays the teachers met to talk over the work and lay out plans for the following week. But there was no obligation to adhere to any plan, and each teacher was placed entirely upon his own. For a time they kept a common diary in which were set down with merciless frankness their failures as well as their successes.

Originality was the guiding spirit. Freedom ruled, but never to the extent of anarchy. When Tolstoy purposely left the room in the middle of a lesson to test the behavior of his students, they did not break into an uproar as he had observed was the case in similar circumstances in classrooms he visited abroad. When he left, the students were enjoying complete freedom, and hence they behaved as though he were still in the room. They corrected or praised each other's work, and sometimes they grew entirely quiet. Such results, he explained, were natural in a school where the pupils were not obliged to attend, to remain, or to pay attention.

Tolstoy insisted that only in the absense of force and compulsion could natural relations be maintained between teacher and pupils. The teacher defined the limits of freedom in the classroom by his knowledge and capacity to manage. And the pupils, Tolstoy wrote, should be treated as reasoning and reasonable beings; only then would they find out that order was essential and that self-government was necessary to preserve it. If pupils were really interested in what was being taught, he declared, disorder would rarely occur, and when it did, the interested students would compel the disorderly ones to pay attention.

The successful functioning of such a school demanded unusual ability on the part of the teacher. Tolstoy admitted this, and justly claimed for himself a certain pedagogic tact. Always in his mind was the pupil's convenience in learning and not the teacher's in teaching. He argued that there was no best method in teaching a subject; the best method was that which the teacher happened to know best. That method was good which when introduced did not necessitate an increase of discipline, and that which required greater severity was bad. The method should develop out of the exigencies of a given problem in teaching, and it should please the pupils instead of the teacher. In short, teaching, according to Tolstoy, could not be described as a method; it was a talent, an art. Finality and perfection were never achieved in it; development and perfecting continued endlessly.

In this free atmosphere of student-dominated learning, certain traditional subjects were resisted in a manner that led Tolstoy to doubt their ultimate usefulness and to question the desirability of teaching them to youngsters. Grammar was such a subject. Although his emphasis in instruction favored analysis, the kind involved in grammar put the students to sleep. To write correctly and to correct mistakes made by others gave his pupils pleasure, but this was only true when the process was unrelated to grammar. After much experimentation with teaching the subject, he concluded in an article in *Yasnaya Polyana* that "grammar comes of itself as a mental and not unprofitable gymnastic exercise, and language—to write with skill and to read and understand—also comes of itself."

In the pages of his educational magazine, Tolstoy provides vivid accounts, filled with all the charm of his realistic art, of daily life at the school. On a cold winter morning the bell would ring. Children would run out into the village street. There was no lagging on the way, no urge to play the truant. Each child was eager to get there first. The pupils carried nothing in their hands, no homework books or exercises. They had not been obliged to remember any lesson. They brought only themselves, their receptive natures, and the certainty that it would be as jolly in school that day as it had been the day before.

At the end of a lesson Tolstoy would announce that it was time to eat and play, and, challenging them to race him out-doors, he would leap downstairs, three or four steps at a time, followed by a pack of screaming laughing children. Then he would face them in the snow and they would clamber over his back, desperately striving to pull him down. He was more like an older brother to them and they responded to his efforts with devotion and tireless interest. Their close, even tender, rela-tions are touchingly reflected in one of the magazine articles. He describes how, after school, he accompanies several of the pupils home on a moonless winter night by a roundabout way through the woods, entertaining them with tales of Caucasian robbers and brave Cossacks. The youngest, a ten-year-old boy, furtively clasps two of his teacher's fingers during the most fearful part of a story. At the end of the narration, by one of those quick transitions of children, an older pupil suddenly asks why do they have to learn singing at school? "What is drawing for?" Tolstoy rhetorically asks, puzzled for the moment about how to explain the usefulness of art. "Yes, why draw figures?"—another queries. "What is a lime tree for?" a third asks. At once all begin to speculate on these questions, and the fact emerges that not everything exists for use, that there is also beauty, and that art is beauty.

"It feels strange to repeat what we said then," Tolstoy writes, "but it seems to me that we said all that can be said about utility, and plastic and moral beauty." The ten-year-old was the last of the group to be delivered to his home. He still clung to Tolstoy's hand, out of gratitude it seemed, and as he entered the miserable thatched hut of his poverty-stricken parents, in which his father and the drunken village tailor were gambling, the lad said pathetically: "Good-by! Let us always have talks like this!"

Tolstoy ended this account in his article by meditating on the age-old question of the moral and practical utility of educating the masses. The cultured, he wrote, would remonstrate: Why give these poor peasant children the knowledge that will make them dissatisfied with their class and their lot in life? But such a peasant boy, concluded Tolstoy, addressing the upper class, "needs what your life of ten generations unoppressed by labor has brought to you. You had the leisure to search, to think, to suffer—then give him that for which you suffered; this is what he needs. You, like the Egyptian priest, conceal yourself from him by a mysterious cloak, you bury in the earth the talent given to you by history. Do not fear: nothing human is harmful to man. Do you doubt yourself? Surrender to the feeling and it will not deceive you. Trust in his [the peasant boy's] nature, and you will be convinced that he will take only that which history commanded you to give him, that which you have earned by suffering."

4

The question of art and its relation to his young peasant pupils interested Tolstoy. With his customary freshness, attention to detail, and marvelous power of direct vision he discussed the subject in one of his most remarkable articles, "Who Should Teach Whom to Write, We the Peasant Children or the Peasant Children Us?" It was inspired by an exciting experience in composition in his school. Themes on the usual subjects, such as descriptions of a forest, a pig, or a table, drove the children to tears. Tolstoy then suggested that they write a story on peasant life, to illustrate a proverb. The pupils found this difficult too, but one boy proposed that Tolstoy write the story himself, in competition with them. He composed several pages and then was interrupted by Fedka, who climbed on the back of his chair and read over his shoulder. Tolstoy explained the plot of the story and the boys immediately became interested. They criticized what had been done and suggested different ways of continuing. Fedka took the leading part in this discussion and surprised Tolstoy by his imagination and sense of proportion, important qualities in every art. Tolstoy set to work to write to the dictation of his pupils Syomka and Fedka, who angrily rejected superfluous details offered by others and eventually took command of the situation. The rest of the boys went home.

Tolstoy described how he and his two pupils worked feverishly from seven in the evening till eleven. Neither hunger nor weariness bothered them. In his account of their collective effort, he gave a number of convincing examples of the artistic rightness and fitness of details, descriptions, and selection that the boys argued and insisted upon. They drew from their experience of village life and characters; and they were nearly always right. Tolstoy was tremendously excited and admitted that he had felt such a strong emotion only two or three times in his life. He was amazed at his discovery of such artistic and creative powers in two peasant lads who could scarcely read or write, and it seemed almost offensive that he, a nationally known author, was virtually unable to instruct these eleven-year-old pupils in his art.

The next day, and still a third day, they continued the story with equal enthusiasm. Then the work was interrupted because Tolstoy had to go away for a few days. During his absence a craze for making popguns out of paper swept the school, and the unfinished manuscript of the story was unwittingly sacrificed to this childish diversion. When Tolstoy discovered the loss upon his return, he was deeply chagrined. Fedka and Syomka, aware of his keen disappointment, offered to reproduce the tale themselves. They came after school one evening at nine o'clock and locked themselves in his study. Tolstoy listened at the door and heard them laughing. Then all grew quiet, except for subdued voices discussing the story, and the scratching of a pen. At midnight he knocked and was admitted. Fedka still had a few more sentences to dictate to Syomka, who stood at the large table busily writing, his lines running crookedly across the paper and his pen constantly stabbing at the inkpot. At last Tolstoy took the copybook. After a merry supper of potatoes and kvas, the boys lay down on their sheepskin coats under the writing table, and until sleep overtook them, their healthy, childish laughter rang through the room.

Tolstoy read the story over and found it very similar to the original draft. Some new details had been added, but the tale contained the same truth, measure, and feeling for beauty of the first version. Under the title of the Russian proverb, "The Spoon Feeds, but the Handle Sticks in the Eye," he printed it, with very few changes, in his pedagogical magazine.

From this unusual experiment in composition Tolstoy drew some interesting conclusions. He declared that nearly all contemporary art was intended for people of leisure and artificial training and was therefore useless to the masses, whose demand for art was more legitimate. He dismissed with some vexation the stale notion that in order to understand and appreciate the beautiful a certain amount of preparation was necessary. "Who said this?" he asked in his magazine account of the writing of the story. "Why? What proves it? It is only a dodge, a loophole to escape from the hopeless position to which the false direction of our art, produced for one class alone, has led us. Why are the beauty of the sun, of the human face, the beauty of the sounds of a folk song, and of deeds of love and self-sacrifice accessible to everyone, and why do they demand no preparation?"

Tolstoy's position was no doubt extreme, and there was also considerable exaggeration in his unqualified praise of the literary ability of his pupils, who were unquestionably inspired by his own artistic interests. Yet such schoolboy efforts helped to teach him the fundamental truth that the need to enjoy and serve art was inherent in every human being, and that this need had its right and should be satisfied.

5

Although the Society for National Education that Tolstoy projected found no support among government officials, his school was not without its influence. After the emancipation of the serfs, the government encouraged them to open their own schools. Peasants in the Tula district, where Yasnaya Polyana was situated, appealed to Tolstoy for teachers, and he willingly suggested a number. By 1862 there were no less than thirteen village schools in his area, and their teachers were all zealous disciples of Tolstoy's pedagogical approach. They caught from him a devotion and enthusiasm in what was essentially a pioneering venture. Living like peasants in the dirty, stuffy huts where they held their classes, and using tables for blackboards, they worked from seven in the morning until late at night. At first, like Tolstoy, they had to overcome the ignorant suspicions of peasant fathers and mothers who distrusted these newfangled methods of teaching and were alarmed because their children were not regularly beaten by the masters. But the fact that they were entirely free to send them to school or take them out overcame resistance. Finally, the happiness of the youngsters and their obvious progress in so short a time eventually won the parent's complete confidence in the system.

In a brief note "To the Public" that introduced his pedagogical magazine, Tolstoy eagerly invited criticism. Much of it was hostile and unconstructive, and particularly that which came from progressive thinkers of the time. He was called a "pedagogical nihilist" and his experiment was castigated as a complete overthrow of educational order and discipline. In a few periodicals, however, several teachers, weary of slavish Russian devotion to foreign models in pedagogy, bravely encouraged the less extreme aspects of his school. But, in general, his efforts failed to inspire enthusiastic acceptance among educators. His principle of freedom for both teachers and pupils was too radical a demand for even the most progressive theorists.

Worse still, in the eyes of critics, was Tolstoy's conviction that his educational ideas amounted to a revolt against established opinion in the name of healthy common sense. Moreover, he scorned scientific exposition in his articles and used the simple and forceful prose of which he was a master. If he had elected to write treatises on experimental pedagogy in the accepted trade jargon, buttressed with elaborate footnotes and well-chosen citations from approved authorities, he would doubtless have gained a hearing, even if an unfavorable one.

As a matter of fact, certain government officials regarded Tolstoy's activities in education with dark suspicion. In October, 1862, the Minister of the Interior wrote to the Minister of National Education to complain about the harmful aspects of the pedagogical magazine. He pointed out that its general direction and spirit perverted the fundamental values of religion and morality, and he suggested that the censor's attention should be specifically directed toward correcting the situation.

In part, the fears of the Minister of the Interior were correct: Tolstoy's educational articles did call into question the whole contemporary concept of morality. His extremely radical position represented a danger not only to the whole foundation of educational practice, but to the authority of the State. The freedom that he advocated seemed to verge on rebellion, and children educated in this spirit would hardly grow up with proper reverence for those institutions of tsarist government that had been infested by corruption and oppression. His educational philosophy would place the human worth and well-being of the individual above the well-being of the State. In short, the spirit of Christian anarchy that Tolstoy was later to preach so openly and eloquently had already crept into his thinking. For in his educational articles he condemned the false morality of government and society, their despotism, the use of force, and the belief in the legality of punishment. And he frankly stated his belief that the masses could exist without the educated classes, and hence without government, but that the educated classes could not exist without the masses.

Because of his marriage, various discouragements, and a suddenly renewed interest in fiction writing, Tolstoy abandoned his school and the pedagogical magazine at the end of 1862. But his concern for the education of the young, which soon revived when his own children came along, remained with him for the rest of his life, as frequent references to it in letters and in his diary indicate. For example, in 1872 he published his first *ABC Book*, in which, he said, he had put more work and love than in anything else he had done. It contained a complete curriculum for beginning pupils. There are sections on reading and writing, with drawings, exercises, and various typographical devices to aid in spelling and pronunciation; there are also sections on natural sciences and arithmetic. He realized the importance of effective examples and exercises, and his selections are original and often reveal rare artistic taste. The frame of reference is restricted by the limitations of the students and their daily lives. "From the natural sciences," he wrote a friend, "I did not choose what may be found in books or anything that I by chance knew or what appeared to me necessary to know, but only that which was clear and beautiful, and when it seemed to me insufficiently clear and beautiful, I tried to express it in my own way." Several of the stories used as examples in the *ABC Book* are entirely Tolstoy's own; others are drawn from various folk sources.

The *ABC Book*, based upon pedagogical theories that Tolstoy had developed and put into practice in his village school, was designed, as he said, for the teacher who loved both his calling and his pupils. The work firmly eschews useless or erudite knowledge, or facts beyond the comprehension or experience of beginners. For the chief significance of teaching, he maintained, was not in the assimilation of a known quantity of information, but in awakening in students an interest in knowledge.

Tolstoy was sadly disappointed at the reception of the *ABC Book*, in which he had deliberately tried to avoid extremes in his theorizing. However, the innovations infuriated pedagogues, and a deluge of sharp, even vicious, reviews resulted. The reviewers charged that the work was an attack on accepted methods of instruction, that he had opposed to a pedagogical system of reason one of faith, to a system of science one of instinct and imagination, and to a system of conviction and ideas one of moral principles. Stubbornly he turned once again to teaching peasant children in his district, in order to demonstrate the methods he advocated in his *ABC Book*.

In 1873 an invitation from the Moscow Committee on Literacy to explain his educational system to them again aroused Tolstoy's conviction that he had a national public service to perform in education. One result of the meeting was a request to test his ideas on teaching, in several subjects, against the conventional methods employed in the schools. Two groups of Moscow children of similar ages and social backgrounds were provided. One of Tolstoy's experienced Yasnaya Polyana teachers instructed a group, and a teacher designated by the Moscow Committee on Literacy the other. At the conclusion of seven weeks of teaching, six members of the committee examined both groups of students. Although there was no unanimity among the examiners, a majority decided that the pupils taught by Tolstoy's opponent had excelled in all three subjects—reading, writing, and arithmetic.

Tolstoy felt that the test had failed to prove anything because it had been conducted under the worst possible conditions. And he submitted the article previously mentioned, "On National Education," to the popular magazine, *Notes of the Fatherland*. It is in the form of a letter addressed to the head of the Moscow Committee on Literacy. The article (September, 1874) is largely a reaffirmation of the views Tolstoy expressed in the pages of his own pedagogical magazine twelve years before. With ruthless dogmatism he condemns outright the phonetic and visual methods of teaching then used in Russian elementary schools. And those native teachers who burned incense to German pedagogical theory he sharply criticized for failing to understand or respect the educational needs of the Russian masses. All a teacher has to know, he declares, is what to teach and how to teach. To find out what to teach, one must go to the people, to the students and their parents. At present, he asserts, the people demand that their children learn how to read and write and to cipher. Until they demand something more, teachers have no right to teach more. As for how to teach, he sums it up in his old phrase: the only criterion for pedagogy is freedom, the only method is experience.

The article created a great stir among the public, infinitely more so than all of Tolstoy's publications on educational themes in the past. To be sure, the work was attractively written, but now it had also come from the pen of the famous author of *War and Peace*, and he had had the good sense to print it in a widely read periodical. In a real sense the effort suddenly made the public pedagogically minded and inspired a surprisingly large number of articles and letters in a variety of magazines. Although the experts, with few exceptions, vigorously attacked him, his views elicited widespread sympathetic response among laymen. After years of striving he at last had the satisfaction of knowing that his theories had reached the general public.

With such encouragement, Tolstoy felt impelled to try for further success. In February, 1875, he published his *New ABC Book*. It was shorter, cheaper, more practical, and, as he remarked in the foreword, adaptable to any method of teaching. Here, too, he now won success, for the Ministry of National Education recommended the work. It was widely adopted by schools and ran into many large editions (100,000 copies were printed for the 1900 edition).

At the same time, Tolstoy published four children's *Readers*, which contained material taken mostly from his first *ABC Book*. The excellence and variety of the selections, the artistic simplicity of the narratives, and no doubt the inexpensive price gained an enormous market for these little books, and over the years they sold in tens of thousands.

Tolstoy's old dream seemed on the point of realization—he was beginning to exercise a pronounced influence on the course of elementary education in Russia. And the dream expanded. He wanted to take a prominent place in the larger field of national education, and he wrote to the minister to inquire whether the government would consider a detailed program that he was contemplating on instruction in the schools and another for training teachers. Although the reply was favorable, it was delayed so long that the impatient Tolstoy had already charged off in another direction. Breaking a rule he had set up for himself, he accepted election to the County Council and an appointment to its Education Committee.

One naturally thinks of the poet Matthew Arnold, inspector of schools in England at this time. With Arnold, however, the post was a means of livelihood and a most unpoetic business. Tolstoy, in his more restricted sphere, found a world of poetry in the work of inspecting local schools. He agitated with some success for inexpensive instruction in the district, and he launched his pet project of establishing at Yasnaya Polyana a teachers' training seminary, for he wished to train peasant teachers to take their place in the milieu in which they had grown up and to provide the kind of education for peasant children that would not instill in them alien desires or render them unfit for the performance of duties to which they would be called by their position in life. This was to be, he remarked, a "university in bast shoes."

In 1874 the Ministry of Education approved Tolstoy's carefully prepared plan for a teachers' training seminary. And his request to the Tula government for financial assistance in return for a certain number of tuition teaching scholarships was granted. But for some unexplained reason, perhaps because educational centers in the Tula government did not favor the idea, only twelve candidates applied for the program. This poor showing discouraged Tolstoy and he refused to open his "university in bast shoes." It was his last constructive effort to improve formal education in Russia. A long and arduous chapter in the history of Tolstoy's civic conscience had come to an end.

Despite hostility to Tolstoy's educational practices and writings during his lifetime, since then there has been a tendency to acclaim him a brilliant innovator and one of the most significant of educational reformers. Experimental schools in America and abroad have profited from the full accounts he left of his own experiences. His methods of teaching the alphabet and reading, his insistence on self-reliance by obliging students to do manual labor, and his belief that the child should be allowed as much freedom as possible in the classroom—these features of his system have had their influence in later progressive education. And one of his principal theses, that the school should always remain a kind of pedagogical laboratory to keep it from falling behind universal progress, has found wide acceptance as an educational premise.

In one respect it may be said that his first absorbing educational experiment between 1859 and 1862 fulfilled another purpose: the school at Yasnaya Polyana contributed as much to the historical development of Tolstoy as it had to the education of peasant children—it brought him back to the career of fiction writing. It was as though a kind of catharsis had been effected that once again left his mind and spirit free for artistic work.

I V

WAR AND PEACE

I

The desire to write a novel about the historical past occurred to Tolstoy shortly before his marriage. Its hero was to be a participant in the Decembrist Revolt of 1825 who, in 1856, returned to Russia from exile. Tolstoy took up this theme in 1863 and wrote three vivid chapters and then put them aside because he felt it necessary to study the period of his hero's youth. The realization that the Decembrist conspiracy had its roots in events connected with Napoleon's invasion of Russia, historical accounts of which had long interested Tolstoy, brought about a new concentration on this earlier period. For in the autumn of 1863 he wrote a close friend that he was absorbed in a novel "covering the years from 1810 to 1820" (actually *War and Peace* extends chronologically from 1805 to 1820). A discarded early foreword suggests that originally Tolstoy may have had a trilogy in mind, in which *War and Peace* would be followed by a sequel focused on the events of 1825 and another on 1856. As additional support for this conjecture, one may cite the "open" ending of *War and Peace*, where Pierre Bezukhov has already begun to manifest an interest in the political movement which five years later culminated in the Decembrist Revolt. There is clear evidence that in 1877 Tolstoy returned to the design of the second volume of the trilogy, "The Decembrists," and actually began work on it. He appears to have had in mind a novel of the dimensions of *War and Peace*. Historical materials were collected and investigated; old Decembrists were visited and their memories of years of proud suffering in exile were ransacked at his request; and Tolstoy went to Petersburg to inspect the dungeons of the Petropavlov Fortress, where some of the rebels had been confined—he was told politely that he could see every part of the prison except the dungeons, which only three persons in the whole Empire, the emperor, the commandant, and the chief of the gendarmes, could leave after having once entered. His interest continued until January, 1879, when he dropped the subject. This decision was no doubt prompted partly by the fact that the authorities refused him permission to study materials in the state archives, and partly because he lost sympathy with the rebel cause when he learned that the movement was not a purely national one but had been inspired by French example and thought.

From the outset of *War and Peace*, Tolstoy was concerned with Napoleon's struggle against Russia and its relation to historical problems, as well as with the peaceful elements of family life, but early drafts and notes fail to indicate that at this stage he had worked out a comprehensive plan that would involve the vast epic sweep and elaborate philosophy of history of *War and Peace*. Nor did the publication in a magazine in 1865 of the first thirty-eight chapters under the simple title *1805*, corresponding roughly to the first twenty-five chapters of the definitive text, suggest that he had hit upon his larger and final design. By the next year, when a second installment appeared which took the story only through 1805, Tolstoy's design did not seem to carry the action beyond Napoleon's retreat from Moscow. Notes at this point hint that the ending was to be a happy one—Prince Andrew, who recovers from his wound, nobly gives up his love for Natasha in order that she may marry Pierre, whose changed outlook on life is uninfluenced by Platon Karataev's simple philosophy; and Sonya, inspired by Prince Andrew's renunciation, gives way to Princess Mary's love for Nicholas. Pierre and Nicholas marry on the same day, and Nicholas and Prince Andrew leave to rejoin their army units. In fact, in 1866 Tolstoy was confident he would finish the novel the next year and publish it as a whole under the title *All's Well That Ends Well!* *

We have no certain knowledge of just when Tolstoy's preliminary and inconclusive plans were brought into focus on a final vision of vaster design and inner harmony, the details of which were undoubtedly developed as the writing continued. At least one clear indication of the kind of insight that fired his imagination and illuminated the huge potentiality of his subject, while at the same time giving it some direction and aim, is an entry in his diary, March, 1865: "I read with delight the history of Napoleon and Alexander. At once I was enveloped in a cloud of joy; and the consciousness of the possibility of doing a great thing took hold of my thoughts—to write a psychological novel of Alexander and Napoleon, and of all the baseness, empty words, folly, all the contradictions of these men and of the people surrounding them." Further jottings in his diary reaffirm his delight with this purpose and his determination to carry it out. At about this same time Tolstoy attended evening gatherings of Moscow intellectual friends where the subject of philosophy of history was much dis-

---

* For some facts on the chronology of the composition of *War and Peace* and supporting evidence drawn from the drafts and notes on the novel, I am indebted to the excellent study of R. F. Christian, *Tolstoy's War and Peace* (London: Oxford University Press, 1962).

cussed. Two problems often debated were the relation of individual freedom to historical necessity and the factor of causality in history. It is very likely that Proudhon's works, which Tolstoy knew, especially *La guerre et la paix,* were also talked about at these meetings. In any event, by March, 1867, the final plan and title, *War and Peace,* had been decided, but the expanded design prevented Tolstoy from finishing the novel until 1869, almost seven years after he began it.

2

The common complaint that *War and Peace* is devoid of form recalls eighteenth-century criticism of the shapelessness of the Alps. In the first place such a complaint overlooks the unique totality of life indigenous, so to speak, to the novel. Given this fact, one naturally asks: What other form, or what changes in the present one, would have resulted in greater aesthetic unity of design in so huge a work? Of course, the logical answer is that Tolstoy surrendered the possibility of satisfactory form by attempting to do too much in a single novel. However, if he had radically reduced its scope, the work would probably not be the *War and Peace* which so many modern writers of stature have acclaimed as the greatest novel in the world.

A close examination of the structure reveals that a unifying design was worked out once Tolstoy had settled upon the scope and purpose of the novel, although this may be form in the sense that Percy Lubbock defines it in *The Craft of Fiction:* "The best form is that which makes the most of its subject. . . ." Interestingly enough, Tolstoy was convinced that in a work of art, form will be determined by the subject, and he believed that this was true of *War and Peace.*

But what is the subject of Tolstoy's great novel? Many have remarked that it has no subject other than life itself and no single hero. The work has such an immediacy for us that we tend to forget what Tolstoy never forgot, that he was writing a historical novel. He makes this abundantly clear from the beginning in his notes, early drafts of chapters, and in abandoned prefaces. In one projected introduction to the novel in 1864, he declares: "I shall write a history of people more free than statesmen . . . ," people, he pointedly asserts, whose faults go unmentioned in the chronicles of history. A little later he repeats in one of the draft versions: "I have been trying to write a history of the people." Then, in replying to criticism of his friend A. A. Fet, of early published chapters of the novel, he explains that, apart from his conception of the conflict of characters, "I have another conception, a historical one, which complicates my work in an extraordinary way. . . ." This special concern he also mentioned to the historian M. P. Pogodin in 1868: "My thoughts about the limits of freedom and independence, and my views on history are not a mere paradox that has occupied me in passing. These thoughts are the fruits of all the intellectual efforts of my life, and they are an inseparable part of that philosophy which I have achieved, God alone knows with what striving and suffering, and it has given me complete calm and happiness." In short, to write a history of the people, understanding history both as a theory of knowledge and as the principal integrating factor in a vast wealth of material, is the real subject of *War and Peace*.

The difficulty is that Tolstoy had his own ideas, which had begun to spawn as early as his student days in Kazan University, on the so-called truth of history and of historians and on the relations of people and their leaders to the historical process. Aware of the significance of his views for the whole course of the novel, he tried to anticipate both objections and misunderstanding on this score by publishing an article almost a year before *War and Peace* finally appeared. There he defends the artist's treatment of history as contrasted with that of the historian. There are two kinds of actions, he explains, those that depend on the individual will and those that do not. In the historical process, he argues, there is a minimum of freedom of action. That is, the so-called makers of history are fundamentally dependent upon the actions of countless other people and hence to that extent their actions are predetermined.

Among these countless people are scores of character types in *War and Peace*, often simple individuals like Tushin or Karataev, and all of them are connected in one way or another with the famous historical events described. The sum total of their individual actions, so often fortuitous or independent of their own will, contributes more to the determination of these events than the actions of celebrated makers of history. It is important to realize that Tolstoy's theory of history applies to the activities of these numerous fictional characters as well as to the purely historical ones. To paraphrase his lengthy and rather involved statement in the novel, he contends that in order to understand the process of history, one must begin not with a consideration of the deeds of supposed great men, but with the integration of an infinitely large number of infinitesimally small actions, what Tolstoy calls "the differential of history."

If Tolstoy tends to deflate the historical reputations of those who are credited with shaping great events by insisting that the events themselves are beyond their active control, the actions of his fictional characters are conditioned by the same lack of freedom. But these tremendously vital, well-rounded, and intensely real men and women enjoy the illusion of freedom, the full consciousness that they are directing their own destinies. Yet fate, chance, accident, lady luck, or decisions thrust upon them by others often determine crucial events in the lives of Natasha, Nicholas, Sonya, Pierre, Princess Mary, Prince Andrew, and others. Tolstoy wisely avoids arguing his thesis on the limitations of man's conscious will in connection with his fictional characters, which may be one reason why its pervasiveness in the total design is often overlooked.

However, the integration of the Napoleonic campaign into the design of the novel, whose subject is the history of the people, is accompanied by lengthy sections of theorizing about war, its leaders, and the historical implications of their actions. Though opinions differ sharply on the necessity of this extensive theorizing, and on its intellectual quality and connection with major and minor fictional characters, Tolstoy obviously regarded it as of the utmost consequence in the definite plan of *War and Peace*. In this sense these sections are not extraneous and may be considered as necessary and extremely informative. To convey knowledge was for Tolstoy an essential concomitant of the novel.

If it is possible to accept all this theorizing as a vital part of the novel's structure, it is something else again to regard it as a convincing philosophy of history. Tolstoy knew war at first hand and no one would deny that the battle scenes are magnificently described and the characterizations of active figures from plain soldiers to marshals and emperors are unforgettable. Who does not recall the boyish, irrepressible Petya Rostov, full of life and desire for glory in the fury of the cavalry charge, and the next moment lying dead on the field. As the gruff Denisov tenderly turns over the bloodstained body, he remembers Petya's words while generously giving away raisins to his comrades a short time before the charge: "I am used to something sweet. Raisins, fine ones . . . take them all!"

Can such a deed be satisfactorily explained in terms of Tolstoy's conviction that man lives consciously for himself but is an unconscious instrument in the attainment of the historical, universal aims of humanity? A deed done, Tolstoy argues, is irrevocable, and its results, coinciding in time with the actions of millions of other men, assumes an historic importance. In history, he maintains, the so-called great men are merely labels, giving names to events, and like labels, they have only the smallest connection with the events themselves. In the novel,

Prince Andrew remarks that the best generals he had known were either stupid or absent-minded. If Tolstoy can be said to have made a hero of any of the famous generals he treats in the novel, it is the Russian commander-in-chief Kutuzov. In his simplicity, intuitive wisdom, lack of hypocrisy and affectation, and in his conviction of the impossibility of controlling events, Kutuzov takes his place with the innumerable simple and patriotic members of the gentry and peasantry as a representative of the unconscious spirit of the nation which Tolstoy identifies as the true historical force at a time of national crisis. Kutuzov admirably illustrated Tolstoy's theory of war, for his strategy, insofar as he can be said to have had any, is based on the assumption that everything comes to him who waits in war. "Patience and time," declares Kutuzov, are the things that win wars. When in doubt, do not act—that is his great military axiom. And in effect Tolstoy defends this position when he writes toward the end of the novel: "If we admit that human life can be ruled by reason, the possibility of life is destroyed."

If truth does not matter to the literary reader of a great masterpiece of history such as Gibbon's, Tolstoy fully realized that a novel would fail if it did not seem to be historically true, for the reader must believe in the whole of society described in it. What particularly troubled him was the prevailing practice of historians of fixing responsibility for what occurs in life upon individuals whom they call great men and endow with heroic virtues. He insists that history is not a science, that no acceptable laws of history have ever been discovered, and that attempts to explain people and events in terms of causes, genius, or chance are simply the result of ignorance. On the contrary, he says, there is a natural law which determines the lives of human beings no less than all the processes of nature itself; all is ruled by an inexorable historical determinism.

Lapses in factual information and substantial distortions in characterizations of great figures of the past, which in some cases can possibly be excused as artistic license, reflect badly on Tolstoy's philosophy of history in *War and Peace*. But a more significant flaw in his theorizing may be discerned by relating his views to the ambivalence that dominated his whole emotional, intellectual, and aesthetic life. As Sir Isaiah Berlin has pointed out, the contrast between the universal but nevertheless delusive experiences of free will and historical determinism corresponds to an inner conflict in Tolstoy between two systems of values—a public system and a private one. At times his irrational depreciation of greatness in *War and Peace* seems psychologically to have been motivated by his private set of values—a feeling of personal envy of the historical fame of Napoleon—just as his later depreciation of revealed Christianity may have been inspired by a feeling of envy of the historical perfection of Christ.

Though Tolstoy regarded his theorizing as essential to the development of the main subject of the novel, he was too great a literary artist not to anticipate the difficulties it would present to the average reader. He rather humorously pictures such readers in a draft version of the Second Epilogue as exclaiming, after repeated doses of historical and philosophical argumentation: "What again! How dull." And he whimsically adds that this sort of reader is most precious to him, the kind whose criticism he most admires. A second type of reader, he says, primarily interested in the historical sections, will blame him for impugning the reputations of great men. But he defends himself by pointing out that he is writing a history of the people involved in a past that has been misrepresented. For Tolstoy there could be no compromise between art and truth, or what he believed to be the truth. The vaunted higher truth of art he would not accept if he found it to be at variance with what he considered the truth of life.

Once the main theme of the novel is grasped, a history of the people and the manner in which all the elements involved in it are integrated by Tolstoy's theory of history, the basic structure becomes apparent and stands as a refutation of the notion that the work is formless. A history of the people is told in terms of the two broad areas of human experience identified in the title —war, symbolizing the vast world of public affairs, and peace, the private manifold activities of the family. A careful examination of the amazingly rich thematic multiplicity of the novel reveals a deliberate and meaningful series of juxtapositions and alternating contrasts, first between war and peace, and then, within this framework, series of alternating contrasts of scenes, situations, events, and characters under each of these two divisions. In war we have the contrasts between Alexander I and Napoleon; good and bad generals; those who think they can direct the course of events and those who make no pretense at doing so; cowardly braggarts among the officers and selfless, unconsciously brave fellows like Tushin. In the division of peace there are the contrasts between the bureaucracy, cultural snobbery, and cynicism of city life and the simple pleasures of country existence; the cold aristocratism of the Bolkonskys and the gay, simple, indulgent Rostovs; or between these two families, with their true patriotism and tradition of unselfish service, and the Kuragins and Drubetskoys, who place their own advancement, financial or professional, above everything. So attached is Tolstoy to this device of antithesis, which he regards as a touchstone of the reality of things, that he creates a series of contrasting characters, and in a few individual characters, such as Pierre and Natasha, he stresses their constrasting moods and thoughts as important traits in their natures. This elaborate pattern of juxtapositions and alternating contrasts serves to create an illusion of ceaseless movement involving an endless variety of action, people, moods, and thought.

3

It is this incredibly rich variety of life rather than the historical forces integrating it in the grand design of *War and Peace* that

primarily interests the reader, and one suspects that this was
also true of Tolstoy. The aim of an artist, he once said, is not to
resolve a question irrefutably, but to compel one to love life in
all its manifestations. With his belief in the timelessness of
human experience, he did not hesitate to project his own into
the historical past of the novel. When he read several early
chapters in manuscript to a circle of in-laws—the Bers family—and their mutual friends, some in the audience looked
furtively at each other as they recognized, among those present, models of a few of the characters. When Natasha Rostova
was introduced, a friend winked at the blushing Tanya Bers,
Tolstoy's young sister-in-law, known in the family as "the
Imp." And Tanya was delighted to hear the description of her
doll Mimi and the true story of how she asked a young lover to
kiss the doll and then made him kiss her instead. The exquisitely
wrought scene of Natasha's first ball must also have recalled to
Tanya her own first ball at which Tolstoy had been her escort.
Although his wife jealously insisted that she had served as the
model for the unforgettable heroine, and perhaps she did in
certain traits, one has only to read the published diary of
Tanya Bers to observe the striking correspondences between
her image and youthful experiences and those of Natasha Rostova. But the perceptive reader will wonder at how completely
the model is transposed, for the realism, vitality, and pure
beauty and poetry Tolstoy imparts to his heroine belong only
to the transmuting power of art.

In general, Tolstoy drew upon the Bers family and their
friends, as well as upon his own parents and forebears, for a
number of the characters in the Rostov and Bolkonsky families. In early drafts, the name Tolstoy is for a time used in place
of Rostov. In several characters it was a matter of borrowing
prominent features, in others of forming composite portraits
from such sources. Though research in the 1812 period provided most of the historical background and local color he

used, which was not extensive, he also depended on family archives, the existence of his own family on their estate at Yasnaya Polyana, and on the Moscow life of the Bers family for city scenes and situations of the Rostovs and Bolkonskys. On the whole, he distrusted writers who invented "reality" by seeking material outside their own range of experience. When necessity compelled him, he used his imagination, and there is much of this in *War and Peace*, but he always contended that it was more difficult to portray real life artistically than to invent it.

In Prince Andrew may be found some of Tolstoy's own characteristics—family pride, deep loyalty, and a profound sense of honor belong to both. Andrew's sister says of him: "You are good in every way, but you have a kind of intellectual pride," an observation that could be made of Tolstoy. In fact, the moral conflict between Prince Andrew and his intellectual foil and unwitting *deus ex machina* of the novel, the easygoing, generous, and noble Pierre Bezukhov, reflects an important phase of the inner struggle that had been going on in Tolstoy since his youth and would in a few years plunge him into a profound spiritual crisis. The debate between them reaches its climax in that impressive scene on the ferry which is steeped in the soft counterpoint of nature's twilight beauties. Andrew, embittered by disappointments in his pursuit of fame and glory and conscience-stricken over the death of his young wife in childbirth, sees no further purpose in life. Pierre opposes his despondency: "If there is a God and future life, there is truth and good, and man's highest happiness consists in striving to attain them. We must live, we must love, and we must believe that we live not only today on this scrap of earth, but have lived and shall live forever. . . ." Tolstoy, after his religious revelation, attempted to resolve the dualism of his nature—to cease living for himself as Prince Andrew had done, and to accept the moral credo of Pierre.

Another manifestation of this same discord in Prince Andrew's nature, which was also so much a part of his creator's, is revealed in the beautiful scene where Natasha is singing and the Prince asks himself: Why do I feel like crying? Am I not perfectly happy? He is, Tolstoy comments, but he is pained by the terrible discord between something immense and indefinite that haunts his soul and the poor, limited thing his body is. Like Tolstoy, the only thing Prince Andrew was sure about was that there was something precious and unknown within him striving to escape, while the flesh bound him to earth. Only in the remarkable scene of his passing, when he discovered that death was a great awakening, did he get a glimpse of what that something was.

A Western critic once said that if life could write, it would write just as Tolstoy did. Surely some such impression is conveyed by innumerable scenes, especially in *War and Peace*, where the reader's awareness of the author vanishes and life itself seems to take the pen in hand. One thinks of such scenes as that of the impish sixteen-year-old Natasha stealing into her mother's bed at night and smothering her with kisses while she charmingly argues her right to encourage Boris's visits, even though she is not going to marry him; the inexpressible joy of the whole Rostov household upon Nicholas' first return from the front, with Natasha shrieking piercingly as she prances up and down in one place like a goat, and his little brother Petya clinging to his leg, shouting for his kiss: "And me too"; Prince Andrew's involuntary eavesdropping on Natasha's ecstasy at the open window of the bedroom above his over the enchantment of a lovely moonlit spring night: "I feel like sitting down on my heels," she exclaims to Sonya, "putting my arms around my knees like this, straining tight, as tight as possible, and flying away!"; or the captivating episode of the young Rostovs, as Christmas maskers, on an evening sleigh ride to their neighbors, where the joyous festivities lead the hesitating Nicholas into the arms of Sonya.

Such scenes are not designed for bravura effects. They advance the action in important ways and add something to the characterizations of major participants. Natasha's talk that night with her mother results in the rejection of Boris as a suitor; Nicholas on his return home brings Denisov with him which sets the stage for his falling in love with Natasha; Prince Andrew's eavesdropping puts in motion the long train of events that will lead to his proposal to Natasha; and the maskers' Christmas party initiates a series of significant complications in the lives of Nicholas and Sonya.

Tolstoy's techniques in characterization are part of the secret of his extraordinary realism, for one of the most difficult things for a novelist is to reveal the total personality of a character, as a person in real life reveals himself. The revelation of personality in real life comes about over a period of time by slow accretions, by the accumulation of much detailed information and understanding through innumerable small actions and intimacies. This is the logical, the natural way, and a close approximation of it is pursued in Tolstoy's novels. We become acquainted with his men and women as we would become acquainted with real people whom we meet for the first time and about whom our knowledge and understanding increase as our intimacy increases over time and space.

Tolstoy does not confront us at the outset with the familiar lengthy description of a character, nor does he take refuge in the awkward flashback. We are introduced to Prince Andrew, Pierre, Natasha, or Nicholas in a customary setting, as we might be in the case of a future friend in real life. Our first impression of the external appearance is only that which we would see ourselves, conveyed by the author's few brief descriptive sentences. We learn next to nothing of the character's past or personality at this point. But from the reactions and remarks of others—this indirect method is a favorite of Tolstoy—and eventually through the conversation, self-examination, behavior, and actions of the character, spread out over many pages and years, our knowledge of him grows until finally we obtain a complete image. There are no startling or abrupt revelations. Each thought or emotion develops out of another. And in the case of characters with a pronounced moral and spiritual bent, like Prince Andrew and Pierre, their dissatisfaction with life is resolved, if ever, not by the author's philosophizing, but by a combination of prolonged self-examination, reflection, and extensive experiences on the part of the characters. As Percy Lubbock affirms, these men and women never inhabit a world of their own, they seem to inhabit our world. That is, their world never strikes us as an abstract one. They stand forth fully defined with all their limitations of time, place, and circumstance. Tolstoy does not hover over the destinies of his men and women; they appear to exercise free choice in working out their fate, so that what they do seems to be psychologically necessary, even though their consciousness of freedom, in the Tolstoyan sense, is illusory. His psychological insights, like his style, create in the reader a sense of intimacy with the characters, for in his analysis of thoughts, feelings, and actions Tolstoy's points of reference are nearly always the reality of life and not abstractions. "You can invent anything you please," he once said of Gorky's fiction, "but it is impossible to invent psychology. . . ."

Such an approach goes beyond conventional realism and suggests not only Tolstoy's complete identification with his characters, but a genuine love for them. Even in negative characters, he nearly always discovers some good, which was his abiding principle in real life. The reprehensible Dolokhov is tenderly devoted to his mother, and the obnoxious Anatole Kuragin is apparently a brave officer in combat. The artist,

Tolstoy believed, is called upon to portray his men and women, not to judge them. It almost seems as though he lived among the characters he created very much as he wanted to live among his friends and neighbors. "The best way to obtain true happiness," he wrote in his diary, "is, without any rules, to throw out from oneself on all sides, like a spider, an adhesive web of love to catch in it all that comes: an old woman, a child, a girl, or a policeman."

It has been noted more than once that characters actually grow and develop in *War and Peace*. The vivacious child Natasha who runs breathlessly into the living room with her doll at the beginning of the novel, and at the large formal dinner boldly demands to know what the dessert will be, is the same Natasha who fifteen years later, at the end of the book, appears as Pierre's wife, noticeably plumpish and sloppy, anxiously scanning the diapers of her newest born. That is, they are really one and the same person at two different ages and not merely two different ages attributed to a single person, a familiar fault with novelists who project development of a character over a long stretch of years. And Tolstoy shows us all the intermediary stages of this growth as he does with other major figures of the novel.

Though one criterion of the realistic novel is truthfulness to individual experience, what writer, when truth is dull, gray, or commonplace, has not garnished it with the illusion of bright exaggeration. There is a suspicion of this in that appealing and unusual peasant, Platon Karataev, who personifies the slow, patient indomitable will of the people that must triumph because its cause is just and its life entirely one of service. Yet Tolstoy rarely deals in illusion. He deals with life itself, and no matter how ordinary it may be, he makes it interesting without the aid of exaggeration. There are no overtly psychopathic cases in *War and Peace*, no lost weekends, no snakepits, and no undue emphasis upon melodramatic, inpressionistic effects to

titillate the reader's sensibilities. What could be simpler and
more unimpressive than the figures of Nicholas Rostov and
Princess Mary. They have no particular brilliance, no special
abilities, and they do not stand out among the ordinary level of
people of their social class. Yet they are evidently admirable
souls, they gain our sympathy, and we identify ourselves with
them. Tolstoy achieves this effect by bringing out in such
characters what he calls the common sense of mediocrity
which, at crucial moments in their lives, is manifested as a
spiritual power that enables these ordinary people to act nobly.

In an uncanny way Tolstoy adapts his art to meet every
exigency of the human natures he describes. For example, in
the case of Princess Hélène, he wishes to convey the impression of a souless nature, of a woman who dazzles all by her
beauty, but is devoid of any inner passion or moral substance.
The method he uses to create this effect is one of brilliant
externalization. At Anna Pavlovna Schérer's soirée at the beginning of the novel, the vicomte is about to tell one of his
stories and the hostess calls Hélène over:

The princess smiled. She rose with the same unchanging smile
with which she had first entered the room—the smile of a perfectly
beautiful woman. With a slight rustle of her white dress trimmed
with moss and ivy, with a gleam of white shoulders, glossy hair,
and sparkling diamonds, she passed between the men who made
way for her, not looking at any of them but smiling on all, as if
graciously allowing each the privilege of admiring her beautiful
figure and shapely shoulders, back, and bosom—which in the fashion of those days were very much exposed—and she seemed to bring
the glamor of a ballroom with her as she moved toward Anna Pavlovna. Hélène was so lovely that not only did she not show any
trace of coquetry, but on the contrary she even appeared shy of
her unquestionable and all too victorious beauty. She seemed to
wish, but to be unable, to diminish its effect.

"How lovely!" said everyone who saw her; and the vicomte
lifted his shoulders and dropped his eyes as if startled by something

extraordinary when she took her seat opposite and beamed upon him also with her unchanging smile.

"Madame, I doubt my ability before such an audience," said he, smilingly inclining his head.

The princess rested her bare round arm on a little table and considered a reply unnecessary. She smilingly waited. All the time the story was being told she sat upright, glancing now at her beautiful round arm, altered in shape by its pressure on the table, now at her still more beautiful bosom, on which she readjusted a diamond necklace. From time to time she smoothed the folds of her dress, and whenever the story produced an effect, she glanced at Anna Pavlovna, at once adopted just the expression she saw on the maid of honor's face, and again relapsed into her radiant smile.

Here, with these few strokes, Princess Hélène's nature is completely revealed. And her beautiful white shoulders continue to gleam throughout most of the novel. When she appears at Natasha's first ball, however, Tolstoy used this feature to draw a significant characterizing comparison. Natasha's "slender bare arms and neck were not beautiful—compared to Hélène's, her shoulders looked thin and her bosom undeveloped. But Hélène seemed, as it were, hardened by a varnish left by thousands of looks that had scanned her person, while Natasha was like a girl exposed for the first time, who would have felt very much ashamed had she not been assured that this was absolutely necessary." Special features, such as Hélène's gleaming white shoulders, Princess Bolkonskaya's pretty upper lip, and Napoleon's white hands, are frequently repeated, not only to fix the character's appearance, but sometimes to suggest a moral facet of the individual's nature.

This method of externalization used in the case of Princess Hélène contrasts with the internal psychological analysis employed in the characterization of Princess Mary. Her deep spiritual qualities lend themselves to such an approach, for she never appears on the scene without Tolstoy making us feel the peculiar inwardness, the moral goodness, softness, and piety of this woman, whose soul, like her eyes, seems always to illumine her pale and unattractive face with the light of moral grandeur.

In the novelist's business of creating life as Tolstoy envisaged it in *War and Peace*, to convey the ceaseless ebb and flow was central to his purpose. At the end of the book, the old order, represented primarily by mother Rostova in her dotage, has passed or is passing. The present generation, Nicholas and Pierre with their wives Princess Mary and Natasha, gathered at Bald Hills with their children, is set in the ways of married people approaching middle age. Then, of the new generation, young Nicholas, son of the dead Prince Andrew, after listening to his Uncle Pierre's warm defence of political liberals in the capital, murmurs to himself in bed that night: "Oh, what a wonderful man he is! And my father? Oh, Father, Father! Yes, I will do something with which even *he* would be satisfied. . . ." Tolstoy indicates by dots that this last sentence of the novel is unfinished. And so is life, he implies. It will go on and on, just as it had in *War and Peace*.

V

ANNA KARENINA

Turgenev once remarked that the hounds of thought hunted Tolstoy's head to exhaustion. He had hardly finished *War and Peace* when he plunged into a study of German philosophy. Hegel's works he dismissed as a "collection of empty phrases," and he preferred Schopenhauer. But Tolstoy's wife informs us that he soon dropped German philosophy, for it literally gave him a headache. He next turned to a formal study of classical Greek which he learned in three months, a claim certified by his Moscow professor in the subject, and like an arrogant schoolboy he boasted of his prowess in letters to friends. Then for some time a vast epic novel on Peter the Great claimed his attention, but after months of research he abandoned the project because of an inability to enter fully into the spirit of the people of this remote period. Besides, as he said, he had come to the conclusion that Peter was a "drunken fool" and a "syphilitic," which dampened his original enthusiasm for the subject.

As early as 1870, however, Tolstoy had told his wife that he had a new theme for a novel which would concern a married woman in high society who had lapsed morally. "His problem," he explained, "was to represent this woman as not guilty but merely pathetic." An intense and prolonged reversion to his earlier pedagogical interests prevented him from beginning *Anna Karenina* until 1873. By the next year he had the first of its eight parts ready for print. Then the whole thing suddenly became disgusting to him and he again took up his educational work, declaring to a friend: "I cannot tear myself away from living creatures to bother about imaginary ones." An additional factor that interfered with progress on the novel was his mounting spiritual illness so clearly reflected in the last part of *Anna Karenina*, which was finally published in 1878.

The working drafts of the novel, as in the case of *War and Peace*, underscore Tolstoy's infinite concern for artistic questions of form, style, and the realistic presentation of characters. The theme that had deeply concerned Prince Andrew and Pierre—the function of moral responsibility—encompasses the whole action of Anna Karenina. And the planned thematic juxtapositions and alternating contrasts of the earlier novel recur in the new one. The central alternating contrast, of course, is the love story of Anna and Vronsky with that of Kitty and Levin. Within this framework the action involves alternately contrasting scenes of Petersburg high society and that of Moscow, of city life and rural life.

The publication, in Russia, of the several drafts of *Anna Karenina* enable one to follow the fascinating genesis of the novel, with its various transformations and modifications, as it developed in the mind of the author. In the drafts it appears that the prototype of Vronsky was the well-known poet and cousin of Leo Tolstoy, Aleksei Tolstoy, who married his mistress. The story element in the first variant concerns only a husband, his wife, and her lover. And in the second part of the novel in the early form, Anna assumes some of the traits of Leo Tolstoy's wife—both women, one in fiction and one in real life, fear not so much possible rivals, but losing the love of their men because of the disgraceful scenes to which they subject them. The turning point in the genesis does not take place until the third draft when Levin is introduced for the first time. Thereafter the novel becomes the story of two married couples. In fact, Tolstoy's title for the work at this point is "Two Marriages." As was true in the case of the wife of Aleksei Tolstoy, Anna commits suicide because of the persistent opposition of Vronsky's mother to his having married his mistress. Eventually, in the drafts the correspondences with Aleksei Tolstoy fade and Vronsky and his relations with Anna take on the form that we now find in the novel.

Unlike *War and Peace, Anna Karenina,* despite its considerable length, is limited in scope and subject matter, has a definite beginning and end, and preserves an inner unity. All the action is securely tied to the main theme, from the opening, when Anna arrives at the station platform in Moscow, hears of the railroad worker's death under a train, and murmurs that it is a bad omen, to the end, when she commits suicide under the wheels of a train, the helpless victim of a fate foretold by the novel's epigraph: "Vengeance is mine, I will repay."

In an interesting letter to a critic who failed to discern the novel's architecture, Tolstoy seemed deliberately to avoid indicating the main theme of the work: "Quite the contrary, I'm proud of the architecture—the arches have been built in such a way that it is impossible to discover the keystone. That is what I most of all wished to achieve. The structural connection is not the plot or the relationship of the characters (friendship), but an inner link." This link, which is really the main theme, is not hard to guess against the background of Tolstoy's experiences shortly before and during most of the writing of the novel. It is the link that connects the opposing situations of Anna's tragic experience with marriage and the relatively happy one of Kitty and Levin. The whole story of Kitty and

Levin—courtship, marriage, the birth of their first child, and their family existence—is in many respects the story of Tolstoy's early years of happy married life. The theme is that the sanctity of the family can be preserved only by the mutuality of pure love of husband and wife which is achieved, as Kitty and Levin demonstrate, by sacrifice, pardon, and the desire to make each other happy. On the other hand, the family is destroyed when either husband or wife indulges in the egotistic love of affinity, which leads to complete preoccupation with one's personal happiness and, as in Anna's case, to the ruin of her life as well as that of her lover Vronsky.

Anna's tragedy unfolds slowly, naturally, remorselessly, before a large audience of the social worlds of two capitals, of the countryside, and elsewhere. But nearly all the fully realized characters, including the brilliantly portrayed Oblonsky and Shcherbatsky families, are involved in one way or another with the fate of these two star-crossed lovers. For Tolstoy, himself a bit in love with his heroine's large, generous, radiant nature, endeavors to show that she is as much a victim of the hypocrisy of this high society as of her own passion. If Anna had had an affair with a handsome, socially desirable army officer, high society would not have condemned her provided she was discreet and abided by conventions that were supposed to make such affairs permissible. The only one hurt would have been her husband, but this was the generally accepted order of things. Above all, appearances must be kept up. Vronsky's mother thought it entirely *comme il faut* that her son should have a liaison with a charming woman such as Anna; it added a degree of social polish to a rising young careerist. So are Stiva Oblonsky's easy adulteries accepted by his society; only in the case of his wife do they cause a bit of pain, but not disaster.

Anna, however, is no casual adulteress. Her love for Vronsky is a deep and lasting passion for which she is prepared to flout convention, sacrifice her security, leave her husband's home, and compromise him openly. She places herself beyond the pale of her social class, but only because of the manner in which she transgresses its hypocritical moral code. Her real suffering begins, not when she deserts her husband, but when she receives the snubs of her friends. In a happy mood just before the birth of his child, Levin is moved to visit Anna. She receives him with the gracious manner of a woman of good society, self-possessed and natural. He immediately becomes at ease and comfortable as though he had known her from childhood. But after he returns home he suffers a revulsion of feeling and, encouraged by Kitty, he thinks of Anna again as a fallen woman. She is the outsider, shut off from the self-confident life of the family. Indeed, the contrast between the marriage of Levin and Kitty, which moves ever outward to include more and more of society, and the affair of Vronsky and Anna, which leaves Anna in her carriage looking out on a city that has finally exiled her socially, only serves to intensify our sympathy for her plight. It is a measure of the moral balance Tolstoy preserves in his portrayal of Anna that he persuades his readers to judge her severely, but with compassion.

Some critics assert that the one flaw in the characterization of Anna is Tolstoy's failure to motivate her seemingly sudden passion for Vronsky. The charge is that he fails to tell readers anything about her emotional nature before she arrives in Moscow to mediate the family quarrel caused by her brother Stiva Oblonsky's adultery, only to be caught in the web of circumstances that leads to her own adultery. Her falling in love, however, is not sudden, and a careful reading reveals how what Anna regards as a harmless flirtation slowly develops into an irresistible passion, a process which in no sense contradicts anything we know of her character up to that point. The process, as in *War and Peace*, involves the use of subtle details that advance the action and psychologically suggest the emotional transformation taking place in Anna. The first real sign of attraction is seen at the Moscow ball, indirectly, through the eyes of Kitty who is infatuated with Vronsky. Another at the beginning of the novel occurs when Anna mounts the stairway of her brother's drawing room to fetch a picture of her son from her bedroom. At that moment Vronsky is shown into the hall. She looks down from the landing and for a moment their eyes meet. An inexplicable uneasiness troubles both of them. She is caught, as it were, on a staircase between the safety of the family drawing room and the safety of the bedroom where her son's picture is. But she quickly dismisses the feeling as of no consequence. On the train back to Petersburg Anna firmly rejects Vronsky's expression of devotion. She treats the matter lightly, but, significantly, she is vaguely disturbed. Then on arrival she notices for the first time the large ears of her husband who is waiting for her on the platform, and a strange feeling of dissatisfaction comes over her as she introduces Vronsky. That first day home she contemplates telling her husband of Vronsky's declaration, but recalling her rejection of it she decides she has nothing to tell, again a refined psychological detail. That night, however, as she hears the familiar measured tread of the slippered feet of her stiff and pompous husband approaching their bedroom, annoyed with herself she begins to wonder what right Vronsky had to look at him the way he did at the station. Then, as she goes to bed, Tolstoy pointedly remarks: "there was not a trace of that animation which during her stay in Moscow had sparkled in her eyes and smile, but on the contrary the fire in her now seemed quenched or hidden somewhere very far away."

Though the seed had been sown, the affair might have ended there if it had not been for the fact that from the very beginning Vronsky's love for Anna is represented as profound and entirely sincere, and it is made clear that he has dedicated his whole existence to securing her love. Nurtured by his endless attention the seed slowly grows and eventually flowers. Yet Anna's passionate capitulation comes only after long heart-searching into the lost cause of a conventional marriage to a man whose colossal egoism is matched by his utter unrelatedness to the human factors involved in the daily business of living. In devoting his entire life to duty, Tolstoy says of him, he even lacks the human weakness necessary to fall in love.

If there is nothing abrupt or illogical in Tolstoy's handling of the early stages of Anna's love for Vronsky, neither is there anything inconsistent with her total personality in the disintegration of their love, so aggravated by her unreasonable but understandable jealousy. In the midst of a reconciliation, another of those small details signals the hopelessness of going on: "She took her cup, sticking out her little finger, and raised it to her mouth. After a few sips she glanced at him, and from the expression of his face clearly realized that her hand, her movement, and the sound made by her lips were repulsive to him."

Nor is there much point in arguing that Vronsky is inadequate to his allotted destiny of creating so powerful an impression on a woman as fine as Anna. Love, after all, is neither rational nor analytical, and besides, the story of the novel is Anna's and not Vronsky's. Dostoevsky reported that someone compared Vronsky to a "stallion in uniform," an observation that may be regarded as a measure of Tolstoy's failure in the characterization. The passionate nature of Tolstoy's realism may have led him at times to reflect a personal bias in the portrayal of certain characters, such as Karenin, or Napoleon in *War and Peace*. But there is no reason to suppose that he denigrated Vronsky in order to extol Anna. Though he personally disliked the code by which Vronsky lived before he met Anna, he faithfully describes the charm of Vronsky's life, its sense of accepted rules, and the self-confidence that made him so much more agreeable in society than Levin. If Vronsky lacks the life-affirming qualities that Tolstoy so much admired in his heroes, he is portrayed as chivalrous, noble-minded, loyal, and extraordinarily gentle, the kind of perfect cavalier who was initially attractive to such different women as Kitty and Anna.

2

Although *Anna Karenina* is one of the great love stories of world literature, it is a tribute to Tolstoy's infallible instinct for reality that he so successfully keeps overt manifestations of love out of the novel. For profound love between two such mature and refined people as Anna and Vronsky is a secret thing, expansive only in hidden ways. The moral and physical effects of their guilty passion are constantly before the eyes of their world, but verbal expression of it is carefully restrained. Their affection for each other is suggested by some kind of mental telepathy in their chats on indifferent topics, or it is conveyed by hints or implications, but rarely by direct declarations.

Tolstoy's art of individualizing his numerous characters, so evident in *War and Peace*, loses none of its effectiveness in *Anna Karenina*. If anything, he adds to his psychologizing a deeper, more searching moral probing. And even more so than in *War and Peace*, he creates in *Anna Karenina* the baffling impression, which is the quintessence of his realism, that somehow the characters are telling their own stories without the author's interposition beyond that of acting as an occasional commentator. At times this effect seems to be something less than illusory. That is, characters appear to retain their freedom of action and behave in ways not anticipated by their creator, or they act a new part in a new situation without ceasing to be themselves. Tolstoy, for example, relates how once a visitor remarked that he had been too harsh on Anna in letting her be run over by a train at the end. Tolstoy replied: "Pushkin once said to some friends: 'What do you think has happened to my Tatyana [the heroine of *Eugene Onegin*]? She has gone and got married! I should never have thought it of her!' So it was with my Anna Karenina; in fact, my heroes and heroines are apt to behave quite differently from what I could wish them to do!"

And on another occasion he warned critics of the inadvisability of concentrating on separate ideas in a work of art without taking into account their essential connection. An obvious proof of this, he pointed out in a letter, was the suicide attempt of Vronsky: "The chapter describing how Vronsky accepted his part after the interview had long since been written. I began to correct it, and quite unexpectedly for me, but beyond any doubt whatever, Vronsky prepared to shoot himself. Then it appeared to me that this was organically indispensable for what followed."

In the novel no deviations are made from human nature's exacting and often cruel demands. Anna has a premonition that she will die in childbirth. By her bedside at this solemn and crucial time her sour, formal husband and her lover are reconciled. Karenin's forgiveness has an air of finality and Vronsky's conscience seems deeply moved by the realization of the sin he had committed. At this point another novelist might have made a concession to the public's fondness for a happy ending. Dostoevsky thought it the greatest scene in the work, one in which guilt is spiritualized and mortal enemies are transformed into brothers before the spectre of death. Had he been writing the story, this experience would no doubt have profoundly altered the lives of the participants for the rest of the novel.

But Tolstoy knew that life does not resolve intense human passions in this manner. Karenin returns to his office routine and his big ears continue to stick out as before. Vronsky conveniently forgets the still small voice of conscience. As for Anna, who had already sacrificed so much for her illicit love, it was too late to turn back. She had already closed the door to her past life, and besides, a woman with her pride would never have permitted herself to knock at that door.

Throughout *Anna Karenina* one perceives Tolstoy's ability to combine a sense of the accidental and inevitable which is the result not of happy chance, but of the novelist's art. He uses a variety of technical procedures, some of them designed to create a kind of symbolic atmosphere, such as the divorce lawyer who catches moths or the pattern of significant actions that take place at railway stations or in trains. Failure to savor this atmosphere is to miss an important unifying factor in the narrative schema. To some, the symbolic effects may seem too obvious, as in the case of the candle whose light, before Anna's suicide, helped her to read the book of her life and then wavered and went out forever. The force of the passage is not in the rather commonplace image, but in the rhythm and depth of the language, the words of which seem to be uttered for the first time. For rugged and solid grandeur there are few passages to compare with it in Russian literature.

Though each of the contrasting couples, Anna and Vronsky and Kitty and Levin, pursues its separate existence, their stories are closely interwoven, and from the contrast emerges the moral repudiation of society's marriage of convenience. This contrast involves still another one, with moral implications already broached in *War and Peace*—the superiority of the natural life of the country over the unnatural life of the city. Levin has in him Nicholas Rostov's passion for the land and for agricultural activity plus a large increment of the soul-searching and questing mind of Pierre Bezukhov. Kitty is the patient, tolerating wife who accepts life's blessings and sorrows as something ordained by heaven. Though she generously sympathizes with Anna's cruel situation, she believes that there are conventional limits beyond which a married woman could not go without risking the condemnation of society.

On the land, Levin's complex nature flowers, and the urgent

language of the description of his activities could have emerged only from Tolstoy's remembered experiences. There is hardly a passage in fiction more poetic than Levin's meditation in the harvest field. But there is nothing of dream or fantasy about it. It is the poetry of fact, and its imaginative quality, its freshness and youth, again derive patently from Tolstoy's own experiences with nature. However, Levin cannot become a peasant any more than Olenin could become a Cossack. The false education of their level of society prevented this. The desire of such characters to transform themselves, to recover a kind of innocence and to achieve the status of the natural man, was one of the central problems of Tolstoy's life, as already suggested, but the answer to it always evaded him. Indeed, one has merely to read Tolstoy's *A Confession,* written after *Anna Karenina,* to observe how much of himself and his life at Yasnaya Polyana are reflected in the characterization of Levin—his dislike of hypocritical high society and government bureaucracy, his love of outdoor work, and his brooding search for spiritual truth. Levin's strident argument with Koznyshev and Katavasov at the end of the novel, in which he roundly blames the government for forcing the Russo-Turkish War on people who know nothing of the issues, was also Tolstoy's position in this struggle. However, there is a patent incompleteness about the characterization of Levin, for his persistent self-examination, guided by a rejection of conventional moral values, seems at the conclusion of the work to be leading him along the path of a new way of life. And Levin's premises indicate quite clearly that he was groping for the kind of solution that Tolstoy himself sought and eventually discovered in the spiritual crisis that overtook him about the time he finished *Anna Karenina.*

V I

RELIGIOUS, MORAL, AND DIDACTIC WRITINGS

I

When Leo Tolstoy and his three brothers were children they used to play a game which had been started by the oldest, the eleven-year-old Nicholas. He possessed a wonderful secret that would make all men happy, he told them, and he had written it on a little green stick which he had buried at a certain spot by the edge of the road in the Zakaz Forest near their house at Yasnaya Polyana. By performing special tasks, his younger brothers would one day learn the secret. Huddled together in a shelter made of boxes and chairs covered with shawls, the children would talk fervently about the mysterious secret written on the green stick. When it became generally known, they decided, it would bring about a Golden Age on earth. There would be no more sickness, no human misery, no anger, and all would love one another.

Tolstoy never forgot this childhood game which may be said to mark the beginning of his lifelong quest for the secret of earthly happiness. That is, the search did not begin, as is commonly supposed, at the time of his intense spiritual experience at the age of fifty. Throughout his early years and during the period of writing *War and Peace* and *Anna Karenina*, his diary, letters, and even his fiction contain abundant evidence of a preoccupation with religious and moral problems. To cite just one of numerous examples, at the age of twenty-seven he entered in his diary: "Yesterday a conversation about divinity and faith suggested to me a great, a stupendous idea to the realization of which I feel capable of dedicating my whole life. This is the idea—the founding of a new religion corresponding to the development of mankind: the religion of Christ, but purged of all dogma and mystery, a practical religion, not promising future bliss but realizing bliss on earth. I understand that to bring this idea to fulfillment the conscientious labor of generations towards this end will be necessary."

There can be no question, however, that shortly after finishing *Anna Karenina* in 1877, Tolstoy experienced a shattering moral and spiritual crisis which brought him to the verge of suicide. *A Confession*, one of the noblest utterances of man, is the chronicle of his doubts and merciless self-examination. He admitted that he had everything to live for—a loving wife, family, wealth, fame, and good health. Yet life seemed stupid, a spiteful joke that someone had played on him. Why should he go on living, he asked himself? Did life have any meaning which the inevitability of death did not destroy?

In *A Confession*, which he began in 1880 and finished two years later, Tolstoy records the unique and overwhelming personal experience of a man perplexed in the extreme by life's most agonizing problem—the relation of man to the infinite.

The result is a masterpiece of the highest art, comparable to the Book of Job in its terrible human urgency of the need to know, as well as in its wonderful language, with biblical echoes, and its compelling use of parables to illustrate ideas. With courage not devoid of a certain humility he dared to tell cynical unbelievers that religion contained the only explanation of the meaning of life, and to believers in dogmatic and popular religions he declared that the very foundations of their faith were erroneous. With complete sincerity, he made it clear that he was uncompromisingly turning his back on all the joys and fame and magnificent artistic achievements of his fifty years of existence in the search for a new way of life that would enable him to seek moral perfection in service to God and humanity.

In a prolonged effort to formulate the direction and terms of his search, Tolstoy devoted the next few years to an exhaustive study of the works of renowned thinkers and the great religions of the world, especially Christianity. In general, he came to the conclusion that the teachings of the Christian churches consisted of meaningless verbiage and incredible statements which afforded no satisfactory direction to man. But in the thoughts of Christ, corrected as he felt they should be if they were to retain their original substance, he discovered an answer to his question about the meaning of life. To put his conclusion in very simple form: the purpose of life on earth is to serve not our lower animal nature but the power to which our higher nature recognizes its kinship. There is a power in each of us, he asserted, enabling us to discern what is good, and we are in touch with that power. Our reason and conscience flow from it, and the purpose of our conscious life is to do its will, that is, to do good. This is the purpose of life which Tolstoy finally accepted.

In the Gospels, specifically in the Sermon on the Mount, Tolstoy sought light on the practical application of this purpose in daily living. From the commandments he extracted five which, he maintained, were the true utterances of Christ. Set down in brief form they are: do not be angry; do not lust; do not bind yourself by oaths; resist not him who is evil; be good to the just and the unjust. All of Tolstoy's future teaching, as well as his own behavior, were guided by these commandments.

Tolstoy's new convictions drove him into a comprehensive examination of the whole organization of modern society. His findings astonished many and convinced others that he was somewhat insane and government authorities that he was a dangerous threat to established order. To his own satisfaction at least, he proved that modern religious faith as preached by churches amounted to a belief in what one knew to be untrue. The Russian Church replied by excommunicating him. Next the institutions of government came under his lash. The result was their theoretic destruction. For a man who will take no oaths, that is, will not submit his will to another, who will not resist evil by force, and who loves all nations and peoples equally and will not punish the just or the unjust, such a man obviously can take no part in war, be patriotic, or hold property, since force is necessary to protect it.

In essence, during the last thirty years of his life Tolstoy labored mightily toward the realization on earth of the kingdom of God, which for him meant the kingdom of truth and good. He did not demand that men be truthful and do good in order to achieve a personal immortality, but because this was the fullest expression of their own personalities and the only way that peace and happiness could be achieved. He saw in the simple tillers of the soil, the hewers of wood, and the drawers of water a deeper understanding of the meaning of life, of goodness, and of truth. Organized government was for him a vast conspiracy against man, designed to exploit his labor, corrupt his soul, and murder him in the violence of war. He fully realized that the end he sought belonged to a distant millenium, but this did not prevent him from devoting all his extraordinary intellectual and artistic powers to denouncing nearly every aspect of modern society which he considered a violation of the natural rights of man.

2

Tolstoy's writings on these matters were extensive, including at least five full-length books, numerous brochures and articles, and scores of long letters which in effect were formal essays on special problems raised by correspondents. All this writing, and much more of a purely creative kind, went on while he was very busy with many civic and family concerns, with endless visitors from all over the world, and hardly ever free from governmental harassment and persecution. Few of these works were permitted publication in Russia, though most of them were widely circulated in clandestine hectographed and mimeographed copies. The bulk of them were sent out of the country and published abroad, which often resulted in printing errors and mutilated texts. Not infrequently numerous copies of printed foreign versions of such works were smuggled back into Russia.

Though at times contemporary critics lamented Tolstoy's forsaking belles-lettres for these purely religious, moral, and didactic works, in them he never ceased to be the literary craftsman, often the artist, and always the supreme writer. That is, it would be a mistake to imagine that they lack elements of the rich art and vision of life of the master novelist. For the remarkable persuasiveness of the best of these writings depends in large measure on Tolstoy's matter-of-fact imagination and that quality of his fiction which reveals a natural concern for the universal activities of humanity. The ruthless realism and brilliant descriptive powers of his novels are frequently carried over into this non-fiction, and his agonizing search in it for the moral laws that will determine the course of his own life is really a continuation of the intense artistic preoccupation with the moral laws that guide the lives of the great characters of his novels.

So large is this body of writing that only the most significant and representative books and articles can be considered here. The first in point of time is *An Examination of Dogmatic Theology* which he wrote in 1880. It is perhaps the least read of all these works, and undeservedly so, for it is an unusually fervent and compellingly logical attack on revealed religion and especially on the Russian Orthodox Church. He combined with a profoundly religious spirit an unsparing truthfulness. Heedless of personal risk in condemning an all-powerful Church, he sought the truth wherever he might find it.

In one sense, the anarchistic temper of his mind admirably fitted him for an examination of dogmatic theology: he was not disposed to accept anything that would not stand the test of reason. If mediaeval churchmen had sought to believe in order to understand, Tolstoy sought to understand in order to believe. On the other hand, he had the defect of this virtue, for he was inclined to place too much faith in his own reasoning. After a thorough study of the dogmas of the Church, he concluded that they were false and an insult to human intelligence. The Church itself, he charged, supported its tenets by deceitful verbal tricks, and sought merely power instead of trying to fulfil its obligation to spread a right understanding of religion on the basis of Christ's teaching.

Tolstoy next turned to an investigation of the Gospels, for he was mystified by what he considered the Church's distortion of the spirit of Christ's teaching. By accepting literally Christ's injunction in Matthew, "Resist not him that is evil," much that had been obscure in the Gospels became plain to him. For by not resisting him that is evil one will never do violence, never do an act contrary to love, which he decided was the real substance of Christianity. And by a literal reading of Christ's words in the Gospels and the precepts of the Sermon on the Mount, he cut through much of the mystical and allegorical interpretation which he was firmly convinced had distorted the plain meaning of these precepts over the ages. On the basis of this lengthy study, in which he used extensive scholarly literature and the earliest Greek texts, Tolstoy elucidated the five commandments of Christ already mentioned. They represented the core of Christ's teaching, he insisted, and if faithfully practiced would link religion to the daily life of man. So brief a summary of *An Examination of Dogmatic Theology* fails to suggest striking features that characterize this and similar writings of Tolstoy—his lucidity of style, the compact argumentation which is never lacking in effective homely illustrations, and his skill in the use of irony and ridicule.

What Tolstoy had set forth as a personal religious experience in *A Confession* and polemically defended in *An Examination of Dogmatic Theology* is crystallized into the most comprehensive exposition of his faith in *What I Believe*, a book that he finished in 1884. The distilled essence of virtually everything he had written or thought on the subject of religion and his relation to it up to this time is clearly and artistically treated. He approached Christ's teaching as a philosophical, moral, and social doctrine, firmly indicated his disbelief in personal resurrection and immortality which, he insisted, had never been asserted by Christ, and for the first time offered a succinct explanation of the position of nonresistance to evil and his reasons for accepting it. The conclusion he reaches is that life is a misfortune for him who seeks only personal welfare which death in the end destroys, but a blessing for him who identified himself with the teaching of Christ and the task of establishing the Kingdom of God on earth, here and now. He goes straight to what matters most for him—the rules of behavior in people. The Ten Commandments of Moses he regards as instructions for doing or not doing, whereas he seeks commandments that will determine being. Despite the didactic nature of the work, it has a profound human quality because of his ability to share with readers the tremendous inner struggle and intense experience that led him to his convictions.

Convinced by his previous experience with *A Confession* that such a religious work would never pass the censor, Tolstoy attempted a rather familiar dodge in such circumstances. He arranged for an expensive edition of only fifty copies of *What I Believe* in the hope that the volume, apparently not intended for popular circulation, would be certified. The ruse failed. The head of the Moscow Civil Censorship Committee reported that *What I Believe* "must be considered an extremely harmful book which undermines the foundations of social and governmental institutions and wholly destroys the teaching of the Church."

3

Tolstoy's new faith aroused in him an intense interest in poverty and social evil, and he felt keenly that he must do something to remedy the situation in his own environment. For the human misery he observed in the slums of Moscow, where he and his large growing family regularly lived in the winters in order to participate in the social season, struck deeply at the roots of his new beliefs and called into question his way of life. But he first felt the need to inform himself fully of the extent and causes of all this suffering, and in 1881 he spent some time in the Khitrov market district among beggars, human derelicts, and prostitutes. The next year, at the time of the decennial census, he proposed a campaign of organized charity in a stirring newspaper article. His plan was to persuade the numerous census takers to conduct a canvass of the city's poor in the course of their official duties. On the basis of detailed information thus obtained, a complete list of the most worthy cases would be compiled along with relevant data necessary to provide the most effective kind of aid. He even secured a position as an organizer in the census and asked to be assigned one of the worst sections of the city, and the conditions of life he saw there appalled him.

The more Tolstoy worked among the poor and thought of the ultimate causes of all this poverty, the more he lost heart in the practicality of his grandiose philanthropic scheme. He soon began to wonder whether dispensing money was a remedy. Was not money an evil in itself, he asked?

Out of these crushing experiences came his well-known book *What Then Must We Do?* which he worked on for several years and did not finish until 1886. He wrestled with the intricate problems connected with the work, for he felt that upon their solution would depend the justification of his new faith. With overwhelming evidence and irrefutable logic, he stated the case of the poor against the rich. Not content with this, he insisted that such economic disparity inevitably resulted in the moral impoverishment of both classes. Nor did he except himself from the general condemnation of the well-to-do; if anything, he was most severe on what he considered his own guilt.

Tolstoy concluded from his experiences that private or organized charity was not an answer to the conditions of the poor. His investigation convinced him that money does not usually represent work done by its owner, but rather the power to make others work. In the course of theorizing in the book he examined his practices and decided that he ought to consume as little as possible of the work of others in order not to cause suffering and vice. No one possesses any rights or privileges, he asserts, but only endless duties and obligations, and that man's first duty is to participate in the struggle with nature in order to support his own life and that of others. And in general he attempted to abide by this conclusion—in answer to the question of *What Then Must We Do?*—in the future ordering of his affairs.

The vicious economic contradictions of society, Tolstoy explained in his book, resulted from the exploitation by the few of the labors of the many, and at the bottom of it all was poverty. The position was an old one with him, but now he saw it in a new light. Formerly men seized upon the labors of others by violence—slavery; now, it was done by means of property. The division and safeguarding of property, he declared, occupy the whole world. Property is the root of all evil, for it brings about the sufferings of those who possess it or are deprived of it, the reproaches of conscience of those who misuse it, and it causes deadly quarrels between those who have a superfluity of property and those who are in need.

What Then Must We Do? is a unique work which, without benefit of the arguments of Marxian economic determinism, did more than any other book up to that time to expose the tremendous contradiction of poverty in modern society. Tolstoy felt the problem acutely, described its unhappy effects with the skill of a great literary artist, and condemned the causes of poverty with all the moral indignation of an eloquent preacher. The solution he offered, however, is by no means as convincing as his diagnosis of the causes. His outlook was circumscribed by the backward condition of Russian society at that time, and still more limited by his instinctive devotion to his own class. He was ignorant of the changes that developing science, industry, and commerce were bringing about in the economics of capitalism, and this unawareness was rendered virtually incurable by an ethical arrogance that made him all too ready to condemn achievements remote from his own experience. An enemy of progress in terms of modern technical advancement, he oversimplified the complex phenomena of industrial and economic life. That government in its systematic organization of society might logically strive to achieve right-eousness, he emphatically denied. Yet in *What Then Must We Do?* Tolstoy performed a signal service in his frank and fresh treatment of one of the most acute problems of modern times, and his prediction that if the problems were not solved in Russia, "a worker's revolution with horrors of destruction and murder" would ensue, was fulfilled not many years later.

In 1886 Tolstoy wrote one of his long letters in the form of an essay on the subject of life and death. The theme gripped his attention and he decided to elaborate it in a book. Through-out most of 1887 he could think of little else. He attended meetings of the Moscow Psychological Society, perhaps with the hope that his ideas on life and death would obtain some support from such learned men. At one of the meetings he read a paper on "Life's Meaning," but his effort was not well received by these disciples of the new materialism.

He finished *On Life* in 1887—Tolstoy used this short title because in the final version of the work he devoted little space to the theme of death. Though it is an important philosophical treatment of his views on the subject, the book is compara-tively little known. All the mature wisdom of some ten years of meditation on religion and on man and his relation to the world is to be found in this treatise, and the beliefs expressed were not significantly altered during the remainder of his life. There is reflected in the work his careful study of church creeds, and he states his conclusion that they consist of incredi-ble statements which afford no real guidance for life. The understanding of life which he elaborates and defends with vigor is that of Christ as revealed in the Gospels, but he avoids the confusion of divergent interpretations of the texts by put-ting his case independently of the Gospels, simply quoting a sentence occasionally by way of illustration. One perceives in *On Life* that he regards all the great religions of the world, which he had studied, as fundamentally one, separated only by the discord among them that man had introduced. The work, like so much of Tolstoy's religious and philosophical writing, admirably exemplifies his absolute faith in reason as the keen knife necessary to cut away all the falseness that has accumulated in religious, moral, and ethical doctrine. It never occurs to him that man may require something more exalted than reason to subdue his inherently iniquitous tendencies.

4

Perhaps the most celebrated and influential of all Tolstoy's books on religious and moral problems is *The Kingdom of God Is Within You,* which he began in 1890 and finished in 1893. It absorbed most of the time he allotted to writing during these years when he was intensely busy organizing widespread relief undertakings to counter the terrible famine that beset Russia. He wrote of his progress on the manuscript to a close disciple: "Never has any work cost me so much effort, or so it has seemed. I want to finish it and yet I shall be sorry to part with it." Of course there was no hope of its being published in his own country, but a Russian edition appeared in Berlin in 1894. When a French translation was submitted to the censor of foreign books in Russia, he is reported to have declared that *The Kingdom of God Is Within You* was the most harmful of all books that he had ever had an occasion to ban. In fact, the government's intensification of its persecution of Tolstoy's followers at that time may be attributed in part to this work.

In *The Kingdom of God Is Within You* Tolstoy carries his Christian anarchism to its ultimate development. The core of the work deals with his theory of nonresistance to evil, which he now applies to governments. He asserts that they are all essentially immoral and exist for the advantage of the rich and powerful, persecuting the masses of mankind through their use of force in wars, in maintaining prisons, and in collecting taxes.

Much of the first part of the book is given over to a consideration of various criticisms of the doctrine of nonresistance to evil while at the same time paying tribute to those who had preceded him in publicly professing this position. A good deal of the criticism had come from foreign countries, but some belonged to native clerical and lay writers, although *What I Believe,* in which he had first advocated nonresistance to evil, had been officially banned in Russia. With a touch of humor he points out that even the government encouraged refutation of a book supposed to be unknown, and that arguments against it were set as themes for theological essays in the academies. Tolstoy also makes the important point in this first part that critics had accused him of preaching moral perfection, whereas he had made it clear that every condition, according to Christ's teaching, is merely a stage on the path toward unattainable inner and outward perfection and is therefore of no significance itself; blessedness lies only in progress toward perfection. He condemns Christian churches of all denominations for perverting the true teaching of Christ in order to maintain their power over the masses upon whom their economic existence depends. Nor does he accept the conviction of many intellectuals that the real import of Christ's teaching rests in its supposed advocacy of service to all humanity. Christian teaching, Tolstoy insists in his book, has nothing in common with socialism or communism or any doctrine advocating universal brotherhood of man based on the advantageousness of such brotherhood. For true Christian teaching, he declares, has a firm and clear basis in the individual human soul, while love of humanity is only a theoretical deduction from analogy.

The contradictions between man's life and his Christian consciousness are dwelt upon at some length. The principal reason for misunderstandings is the acceptance of Christ's teaching without making an effort to change one's life. But recognition of this error, says Tolstoy, is becoming more and more general. "Humanity has outgrown its social and governmental stages," he writes, "and has entered upon a new one. It knows the doctrine that should be made the basis of life, but through inertia continues to keep to the old forms of life. From this discord between the new understanding of life and its practise, a series of contradictions and sufferings results, which poison our life and demands its alteration."

The rest of the book is concerned with an examination of the powers and activities of governments that enable them to prevent the masses of mankind from resolving, in favor of Christ's teaching, the contradictions between their present life and their Christian consciousness. Force or violence he singles out as the chief instruments that governments employ to maintain themselves in power and the people in subjection to the un-Christian life thrust upon them. Every manifestation of governmental force is analyzed by Tolstoy, especially military conscription and war. The result is one of the most scathing denunciations of war ever written.

Nor does Tolstoy accept revolution as a way out of the tyranny of governments. He was unalterably opposed to its violence, and besides, history had taught him that in such forcible changes the masses are the sufferers and that under the new government oppression in no way lessens but sometimes even increases. Only people who have something which they will under no circumstances yield, he argues, can resist a government and curb it. The way out, he urges, is passive, civil disobedience to all those demands of government which violate the conscience of men. For only thus will public opinion, the sole power that can subdue governments, be aroused. And only men who live according to their conscience can exert influence on people, and only activity that accords with one's conscience can be useful.

In short, the escape from the violence and oppression of governments, Tolstoy concludes in this book, is for all mankind to live according to the true precepts of Christ. Man must understand, he declares, that "his life does not belong to himself or his family or the State but to Him who sent him into the world, and that he must therefore fulfill not the law of his personality or family or State, but the infinite law of Him from Whom he has come—and he will feel himself absolutely free from all human authorities and will even cease to regard them as able to trammel anyone."

Nor did Tolstoy hesitate to blueprint in his book the way of salvation for the man who is aroused to an understanding of true Christianity. His first precept is to remember that the only guide for a Christian's actions is to be found in the divine principle that dwells within him, which in no sense can be checked or governed by anything else. Man must not suppose, Tolstoy insists, that the amelioration of life will come about, as the socialists preach, by some spontaneous, violent reconstruction of society. The freedom of all men can be achieved only by the liberation of individuals separately. Every man, hearkening to the dictates of his conscience and abiding by the teaching of Christ, must quietly refuse to serve the government in any way: he must refuse to take an oath, to pay taxes, or to serve in the army. If he is persecuted for thus violating the law, he must not oppose violence by force.

Without explicitly stating it in his book, Tolstoy quite clearly anticipated a growing movement of civil disobedience based on the principle of nonresistance to evil, which he was convinced would eventually undermine the whole structure of government. He believed that such a forward movement of humanity toward a more conscious assimilation of the Christian conception of life already existed. This moral progress, he felt, would ultimately influence public opinion, and once such informed public opinion gained ascendancy, it would transform all the activity of men and bring it into accord with Christian consciousness. Then truly would the Kingdom of God on earth be achieved by every man first realizing that the kingdom was within himself.

It is impossible to convey in a necessarily short analysis the persuasiveness of Tolstoy's closely reasoned arguments, running over almost five hundred pages of this work, and there is also the danger of minimizing its effectiveness, for he rarely fails to anticipate objections to his solutions of the many controversial issues he raised. But the fault he committed in all his didactic works, that of generalizing on the basis of special conditions existing in Russia, is everywhere in evidence in the book. There was a manifest unfairness in his failure to give credit to democratic progress in governments of Western Europe and America, although he bluntly declared that the only difference between a despotic government and the republics of France and America was that, in the former, power was concentrated in the hands of a small number of oppressors and the violence was cruder, whereas in the latter, power was divided among a larger number of oppressors and was expressed less crudely.

5

There is bound to be a certain arbitrariness in attempting to select for brief comment what appear to be the most significant of the shorter pieces belonging to this chapter. For the purpose of convenient thematic reference, as well as for observing the scope and development of Tolstoy's views on the subject matter indicated, it seems best to arrange these articles under three broad headings. In the first, on religion, the separate "Preface" to his unfinished *The Christian Teaching* (1898), an attempt to state his religious perception in systematic form, recapitulates in a concise manner the doubts and difficulties Tolstoy experienced in arriving at his beliefs. In essence it is a kind of later summary of the detailed account in *A Confession* and hence provides an effective brief introduction to his whole treatment of religion.

In "Religion and Morality" (1893) Tolstoy examines several religions in an effort to answer the frequent query of what religion is and whether morality can exist independently of it.

He concludes that the relation which man establishes between his individual personality and the infinite universe or its source is religion, and that it cannot exist apart from morality, which is an outgrowth of this relation and the ever-present guide to life.

Tolstoy's rationalism, his emphasis on the primacy of reason in any concern with faith, is stressed in the succinct treatment of "Reason and Religion." The purpose of this epistolary essay is to demonstrate that man has received direct from God only one instrument wherewith to know himself and his relation to the universe—reason. Therefore—the argument runs—it is entirely proper for man to exert the whole strength of his mind to elucidate for himself the religious foundation on which his faith must rest. Here we have Tolstoy, the rationalist, protesting against mysticism or revelation of any sort, a protest that worried certain disciples who were mystically minded.

The "Reply to the Synod's Edict of Excommunication" (1901) is a dignified and impressive rejoinder to the Russian Orthodox Church's exclusion of Tolstoy from its membership. His fundamental differences with the Church had been a matter of public knowledge for a long time before this official separation, but he avails himself of the opportunity to restate his views on the Church and to point out in forceful language why he believes that it is the chief obstacle to those who seek a reasonable understanding of religion.

Though Tolstoy's writings on religion and his denunciations of the practices of the Russian Orthodox Church provided sufficient reason for his excommunication, the action provoked a surprising amount of public sympathy on his behalf. In his reply to the edict he explained in forthright terms what he considered to be true and what untrue in the Holy Synod's statement. He admitted that he did not believe in what the Church said it believed in, and yet he insisted that he believed in much that the Church had attempted to persuade people that he did not believe. "I believe in this," he wrote. "I believe in God, whom I understand as Spirit, as love, as the Source of all. I believe that He is in me and I in Him. I believe that the will of God is most clearly and intelligibly expressed in the teaching of the man Jesus, whom to consider as God and pray to, I esteem the greatest blasphemy. I believe that man's true welfare lies in fulfilling God's will, and His will is that men should love one another and should consequently do to others as they wish others to do to them—of which it is said in the Gospels that in this is the law and the prophets. I believe therefore that the meaning of the life of every man is to be found only in increasing the love that is in him; that this increase of love leads man, even in this life, to ever greater and greater blessedness, and after death gives him the more blessedness the more love he has, and helps more than anything else toward the establishment of the Kingdom of God on earth: that is, to the establishment of an order of life in which the discord, deception, and violence that now rule will be replaced by free accord, by truth, and by the brotherly love of one for another."

After this confession of faith, Tolstoy rose to heights of nobel sincerity in concluding his answer to the Synod: "Whether or not these beliefs of mine offend, grieve, or prove a stumbling block to anyone, or hinder anything, or give displeasure to anybody, I can as little change them as I can change my body. I must live my own life, and I must myself alone meet death (and that very soon), and therefore I cannot believe otherwise than as I—preparing to go to that God from whom I came—do believe. I do not believe my faith to be the one indubitable truth for all time, but I see no other that is plainer, clearer, or answers better to all the demands of my reason and my heart; should I find such a one I shall at once accept it; for God requires nothing but the truth. But I can no more return to that from which with such suffering I have escaped, than a flying bird can re-enter the eggshell from which it has emerged."

Not long after his reply to the Holy Synod, Tolstoy completed a long essay, "What Is Religion, and Wherein Lies Its Essence" (1902). Within its scope, this work is perhaps his most conclusive, best-tempered, and persuasive treatment of the subject. He approaches it historically and reaches a definition of true religion as the relation which man, in terms of reason and knowledge, establishes with the infinite life surrounding him, and it binds him to that infinity and determines his conduct. The real essence of Christianity, he declares, is allied with the essence of all other major religions, whereas faith is neither hope nor credulity, but a special state of the soul that obliges man to do certain things.

6

The second grouping is on peace, a subject that commanded a great deal of Tolstoy's attention during the last years of his life. Here not only his central doctrine of nonviolence is involved, but also his conviction that the amazing advances of science will be used more and more to develop frightful instruments of war to kill millions of people more expeditiously. His vigorous efforts to unmask the social, political, and economic forces that cause war and prevent peace are often most effective, but the remedies he offers appear to defy the logic of civilization's progress, although it must be realized that Tolstoy seriously questioned the validity of what is generally accepted as "modern progress."

The extensive essay "Christianity and Patriotism" (1894) is one of the finest of these efforts and at the same time an excellent example of his polemical powers. He begins with a shrewd and often amusing account, based on newspaper reports, of the outpouring of fraternal admiration and patriotism that gripped Russia and France on the occasion of the exchange of visits, in 1893, of their respective fleets to Kronstadt and Toulon. Then Tolstoy debunks all this manufactured enthusiasm as something contrived by the two governments to enlist public support in case war breaks out between France and Germany. He indicts patriotism as a false sentiment and demonstrates that it and war have nothing in common with the true interests of the masses or with the precepts of Christianity.

"Patriotism and Government" (1900) is a shorter and more angry article, prompted by the cynicism of the peaceful professions of the great powers at the very time they are planning further strife. To deliver mankind from the ever-increasing evils of growing armaments and war, Tolstoy argues, neither congresses nor conferences nor courts of arbitration will do; simply destroy those instruments of violence called governments from which humanity's greatest evils flow. To eliminate the violence of governments only one thing is needed: people should be made to realize that the feeling of patriotism, which supports violence, is a bad feeling, and, above all, is immoral. It can be eradicated, he points out, only when men are educated through Christ's teaching that it is wrong to kill. And he prophetically anticipates more terrible wars—World War I began fourteen years later—unless universal disarmament can be achieved.

Tolstoy accepted an invitation to participate in the Eighteenth International Congress for Peace at Stockholm in August, 1909, although earlier he had repeatedly refused to attend such gatherings. He now felt it his duty to use this opportunity to present his views at a world forum, and he eagerly set to work on his speech. It appears that the organizers of the Congress were more surprised than pleased by his acceptance. They had not expected this feeble old man of eighty to attend and had merely wished to use his name and receive his moral support. Their surprise turned into embarrassment when the news leaked out to the world press that Tolstoy would challenge the Congress to be honest for once and demand the abolition of all armies as the only sincere and effective way to obtain world peace. Because of health and family complications, it was unlikely that he would have attended anyway, but the Congress leaders suddenly announced that the meeting would be postponed until the next year owing to a worker's strike—some newspapers flatly declared that the real reason was the fear that Tolstoy would actually appear and deliver his speech. They had cause to fear, for his "Address to the Swedish Peace Congress" (1909) is one of Tolstoy's strongest denunciations of war and of the governments that perpetuate it. He sees the problem as an acute contradiction between the moral demands of mankind and the existing social order. The moral truth in its full meaning, he declares, lies in what was said thousands of years ago, the law of God: "Thou Shalt Not Kill." The military profession, he asserts, "notwithstanding all the efforts to hide its real meaning, is as shameful a business as an executioner's and even more so. For the executioner only holds himself in readiness to kill those who have been adjudged harmful and criminal, while a soldier promises to kill all whom he is told to kill, even though they be those dearest to him or the best of men." At the end of his address Tolstoy called upon all individual members of the Congress to use the utmost public moral pressure on their various governments to convince them that war is not patriotism or service to one's country but "the naked, criminal business of murder!"

The five commandments that Tolstoy had distilled from the Gospels guided his daily conduct, and his devotion to the Christian ideal as he understood it—a renunciation of one's self in order to serve God and one's neighbor—made of his conscience a watchdog to detect the slightest intrusion of heretical thoughts or actions. In these terms he not only tried honestly to reform his own behavior, but also, through his writings, the moral, social, and political abuses of society. A selection of such articles makes up this final grouping.

At the age of sixty, for example, Tolstoy renounced meat, alcohol, and tobacco. That year he wrote his article, "Why Do Men Stupefy Themselves?" (1888), in which he roundly condemns drinking and smoking as habits employed by mankind to still the voice of conscience. The peasants of Yasnaya Polyana were among his first converts; they reluctantly surrendered their tobacco pouches and took the pledge not to drink and then broke it by stealth. Though Tolstoy's absolutism in these matters is discouraging, it is interesting to observe, because of his views on nonresistance to evil, that he does rule out the use of force or laws to obtain his ends, compulsions that are advanced and sometimes unsuccessfully employed to eradicate these habits in our own day.

"The First Step" (1891) is really a moral essay on right living and points out the wisdom of moving toward virtue by taking the first step up the ladder on which all other steps depend. The simple way of life which Tolstoy had begun to lead after his spiritual revelation he now advocates as the rational and Christian way for people—taking care of all one's needs oneself and not depending on the labor of others. The last part of the essay is a powerful argument for vegetarianism. Here the novelist's art is employed in a nightmarishly realistic description of the slaughterhouse and its dumb victims, the material for which he gathered at first hand.

Both moral and political questions are dealt with in "Thou Shalt Not Kill" (1900), inspired by an anarchist's assassination of King Humbert of Italy. Here Tolstoy's tone becomes somewhat shrill, and his customary moral earnestness gives way to harsh criticism of the mighty rulers of the earth who cause the death of countless people without arousing the indignation that swept Europe over the murder of a single king. But in the end

Tolstoy draws the moral that it is just as evil for private individuals to kill kings as it is for kings to send thousands of their subjects to death in wars.

In "What's to Be Done?" (1906) Tolstoy attempts to answer the question put by young radicals caught up in the turmoil of the 1905 Revolution. Since the government and the revolutionists who opposed it were both committed to violence, Tolstoy's answer is that all should accept God's law to love one another, but that in any case they should not kill or attack each other's liberty.

None of Tolstoy's many articles and pamphlets on contemporary issues won for him such international *réclame* as "I Cannot Be Silent" (1908), written when he was eighty. The emotional intensity and high seriousness of the piece were no doubt influenced by a long series of police prosecutions of his followers for publishing, possessing, lending, or distributing his anti-government writings. If these acts were crimes, he felt equally guilty, and the fact that he was not punished tormented his conscience. Then, too, the rising incidence of executions of revolutionists and terrorists caused him much anguish. He wrote a friend: "My God, my God, these executions, prisons, jails, these exiles! And they imagine that they will improve something or other." Then came the newspaper report of the hanging of twenty peasants (actually twelve) for attacking a landowner. This was more than Tolstoy could bear and he wrote his famous article, an effort that gave him a feeling of great moral relief. Tolstoy's superb literary talent and his knowledge of human psychology and sense of drama contribute to this impressive and anguished outcry against man's inhumanity. He struck a note that won response from all thinking people. The crimes of the revolutionists, he points out, are terrible, but they do not compare with the criminality and stupidity of organized legalized violence of the government. The delusion is the same in both, he added, and the excuse is that an evil deed committed for the benefit of many ceases to be immoral. Since the government claims these executions are done for the general welfare, Tolstoy declares, then he as one of the people cannot escape the feeling that he is a participator in these horrible deeds. In the end he defies the government, promising to circulate his article by every means in his power, in the hope that either these inhuman punishments may cease or that he may be sent to prison and thus be relieved of the burden of conscience that the executions are committed on his behalf. Better still, he writes, let them "put on me, as on those twelve or twenty peasants, a shroud and a cap and push me also off a bench, so that by my own weight I may tighten the well-soaped noose round my old throat."

VII

WHAT IS ART?

Art is modest, Tolstoy once said, but his theorizing on the subject in *What Is Art?* is perhaps the most immodest contribution to aesthetics ever written. This famous work, which he finished in 1897, marked the culmination of fifteen years of thought and study, a fact unknown or disregarded by captious critics who have treated it as something that leaped full-blown from Tolstoy's brain at a dyspeptic moment when he arbitrarily decided that there ought not to be any more cakes and ale for artists of the world.

Early letters and jottings in his diary reveal that from the time when he first began to write in the 1850's Tolstoy had already become almost morbidly conscious of the techniques of his craft and the perplexing imponderables involved in the theory of literary art. And we have observed that at the end of the 1850's he tried to redefine his relation to art in opposition to the then growing popular trend of social significance in literature, a struggle which eventually disillusioned him with belles-lettres and contributed to turning his major attention to educational theory and practice. But even in that phase of his career it was pointed out that he could not refrain from speculating about aesthetic matters in the course of directing the fascinating experiments of his young students in literature and writing. This reawakened interest in art led him naturally into the creation of those great masterpieces of fiction of the 1860's and 1870's—*War and Peace* and *Anna Karenina*.

Then at the beginning of the 1880's, during his spiritual upheaval, Tolstoy took a full reckoning of his views on art. He came to the conclusion that the art he had served for years was a temptation that seduced people from good and led them into evil. He decided to forsake art. Although he never subsequently found it necessary to surrender his fundamental negative position towards other "deceits of culture"—government, law, science, technical progress, and so on—he soon began to doubt his negative attitude toward art. Art was so intimate a part of his being that he could not entirely turn his back on it.

However, with his radically new outlook on life, Tolstoy could not be satisfied with the view of art that he had formerly accepted, and this dissatisfaction inspired a prolonged study of the subject. His main endeavor was to erect a system of aesthetics that would accord with his new understanding of man and his relation to the world. In a real sense, *What Is Art?* may be regarded as the aesthetic of his new moral philosophy. Yet he understood that any system he might set up must be comprehensive enough to justify and explain all sincere works of art.

The problem turned out to be much more complicated than Tolstoy had anticipated. His first effort was an attempt to write an article for a Moscow art magazine in 1882, in which he tried to formulate a definition of art that would emphasize the importance of a moral and useful purpose in life. He did not get very far and left the manuscript unfinished, apparently conscious of the fact that he had not thought the matter through. But he had actually begun the long train of formal aesthetic speculation that led to his astounding book, *What Is Art?*

In the course of the next fifteen years, over various periods of time, Tolstoy pondered the subject, defining and redefining his position. He read a great many books on aesthetics, philosophy, and works of belles-lettres, and he studied music, painting, and sculpture, attended the theater, and heard opera, always with his projected book in mind. Apart from a quantity of miscellaneous notes, there exist eight separate articles, fragments of articles, and drafts. This material, which has been published in Russian in a special volume devoted to the subject, is almost as extensive as his final effort, *What Is Art?*

In all Tolstoy's theorizing during these years, one can detect a growing emphasis upon the ethical principle as the immanent organizing factor in the artistic process. And this view ultimately became the starting point for the aesthetic theory that he finally elaborated in *What Is Art?* The growing popularity of movements such as those of the Decadents and Symbolists during the last decade of the nineteenth century offended both his artistic and moral sense and provided him with a new impetus to complete his study. He worked almost exclusively on it throughout 1897 and finished in December. It appeared in Russia the next year, but was so mutilated by both the editor and the censor that Tolstoy disowned the work. At the same time, it was published in England in a translation made by Aylmer Maude and supervised by Tolstoy, who declared this version to be the first complete and correct edition of *What Is Art?*

2

In this book, Tolstoy approached the subject as he now approached the study of every human endeavor: art is a human activity and hence it must have a clear purpose and aim, discernible by the aid of reason and conscience. And as a human activity, he declared, art cannot exist for its own sake and therefore its value must be weighed in proportion as art is serviceable or harmful to mankind. Again and again in his researches he was confronted by that unholy trinity of the aestheticians—beauty, truth, and goodness, and of these the greatest was beauty. For he found that the commonest definition, repeated in various forms, was that art is an activity dedicated to the cause of beauty. But just what was meant by beauty, no two theorists seemed to agree. The word was used subjectively according to varying tastes of the persons who employed it. In general, Tolstoy's preliminary study of aesthetics led him to conclude that there was no such discipline, because it failed to define the qualities and laws of art which could in turn be applied to artistic productions by way of accepting or rejecting them. This chaos has resulted, he maintained, because the conception of art has been erroneously based on the conception of beauty.

Tolstoy then propounded his own definition of art:

To evoke in oneself a feeling one has once experienced and having evoked it in oneself then by means of movements, lines, colors, sounds, or forms expressed in words, so to transmit that feeling that others experience the same feeling—this is the activity of art.

Art is a human activity consisting in this, that one man consciously by means of certain external signs, hands on to others feelings he has lived through, and that others are infected by these feelings and also experience them.

Art is not, as the metaphysicians say, the manifestation of some mysterious Idea of beauty or God; it is not, as the aesthetic physiologists say, a game in which man lets off his excess of stored-up energy; it is not the expression of man's emotions by external signs; it is not the production of pleasing objects; and, above all, it is not pleasure; but it is a means of union among men joining them together in the same feelings, and indispensable for the life and progress towards well-being of individuals and humanity.

Before Tolstoy applied his definition as a kind of touchstone of true art, he believed it essential to distinguish between the subject matter and form of art, for he realized that this distinction contained the solution of what was for him the fundamental problem—the relation of art to morality. First he considered art apart from its subject matter and pointed out that what differentiated real art from its counterfeit—and much that passed for art he condemned as counterfeit—was its infectiousness. If a person subjected to an artist's work experiences a mental condition which unites him with the artist and other people who partake of the work of art, then the object evoking that condition is a work of art. And the stronger the infection, the better is the art as art. From this point of view, he declared, art has nothing to do with morality, for the feelings transmitted may be good or bad feelings. But the one great quality that makes a work of art truly contagious, he asserts, is its sincerity.

Up to this point in his book, Tolstoy has been concerned with an internal test in appraising art. He next applied an external test in an effort to determine whether a work of art is refined or genteel (the art of the few, the upper classes) or universal (the art of the people). Those who admire exclusive art, he insisted, which is so often considered the only art, do so because they train themselves to admire it and not because it is necessarily great art. Then he goes on to indicate that the majority of the productions of art of the upper classes, which are admired by them when first produced, are never understood or valued by the masses of mankind. This refined art, he argues, is intended only for the pleasure of genteel people and is incomprehensible as a pleasure to the working men. For almost the only feelings, with their offshoots, that form the subject matter of upper class art, Tolstoy said, are three insignificant and simple ones—the feeling of pride, the feeling of sexual desire, and the feeling of weariness of life.

As soon as the art of the upper classes separated itself from universal art, Tolstoy wrote, a conviction arose that art could be art and yet be incomprehensible to the masses. But all great works of art, he contended, are great because they are accessible and comprehensible to everyone. The majority of people have always had the taste to esteem the highest works of universal art, such as the epic of Genesis, the Gospel parables, and folk-legends, songs, and tales, because they invoke the simple feelings of common life, accessible to all, and yet do not hinder progress towards well-being. Art of this kind, he said, makes us realize to what extent we already are members of the human race and share the feelings of one common human nature.

3

Though thus far in *What Is Art?* one may quarrel with the aesthetics of Tolstoy's position, it compels attention by its originality and consistency. But he provokes sharp reactions from critical readers when he attempts to illustrate his theory. Guided largely by religious and moral convictions, he designates categories among artistic productions in terms of their varying degrees of infectiousness and feelings. In this matter, however, it is well to remember that he attached no special importance to his examples. "I may mistake for absolute merit," he disarmingly admitted, "the impressions a work produced on me in my youth." Moreover, the reader today ought perhaps to make allowances, in passing judgment on the illustrations, for all the conditioning factors of literary taste of an age long past, as well as the educational, cultural, and social background of a Russian nobleman born more than a century ago.

In applying the touchstone of feeling to art, Tolstoy asserted, it is essential to differentiate what are the best feelings and what are evil. Only through this distinction will the intimate and inevitable connection between morality and art become apparent. For if art unites men, the better the feelings in which it unites them, the better it will be for humanity. Tolstoy candidly agreed that the definition of the best and highest feelings will differ from age to age. Each age, he said, has possessed a dominant view of life which may be described as its "religious perception." And the true religious perception of the Christian age is Christ's teaching, which permeates the whole life of man today, and if we accept this religious perception, it must inevitably influence our approval or disapproval of the various feelings transmitted by art. The best and highest feelings of art, then, are those which invoke Christ's love for God and one's neighbor. When this religious perception is consciously acknowledged by all, Tolstoy declared, then the division of art into art for the lower and art for the upper classes will disappear, for art which transmits feelings incompatible with religious perceptions of our time will be rejected.

As examples of this highest art "flowing from love of God and man (both of the higher, positive, and the lower, negative kind) in literature," Tolstoy mentioned Schiller's *The Robbers*, Hugo's *Les Misérables* and *Les Pauvres Gens*, Dickens' *A Tale of Two Cities*, *A Christmas Carol*, and *The Chimes*, Harriet Beecher Stowe's *Uncle Tom's Cabin*, Dostoevsky's *The House of the Dead*, and George Eliot's *Adam Bede*.

Of course, Tolstoy did not limit the subject matter of art to these highest religious feelings, as some critics suppose. He stressed another major division of art, the universal, which conveys feelings of common life accessible to everyone—such as feelings of merriment, pity, cheerfulness, tranquility, and so forth. With qualifications, and only because of their inner content, he cited as examples of good universal art produced by the upper classes, Cervantes' *Don Quixote*, Molière's comedies, Dickens' *David Copperfield* and *Pickwick Papers*, and the tales of Pushkin and Gogol.

But the scope of the artist, Tolstoy said, must in no sense be restricted. The whole world of feelings must be his sphere of activity. Yet he does argue that a folk tale, a little song, or a lullaby that delights millions of children or adults is incomparably more important than a novel or a symphony that will divert some few members of the wealthy class for a short time and then be forever forgotten. Almost untouched, he declared, is this region of art in which the simple feelings are made accessible to all, and like the highest religious art, it tends to unite all mankind. He wrote:

> Sometimes people who are together, if not hostile to one another, are at least estranged in mood and feelings, till perhaps a story, a performance, a picture, or even a building, but oftenest of all music, unites them all as by an electric flash, and in place of their former isolation or even enmity they are conscious of union and mutual love. Each is glad that another feels what he feels; glad of the communion established not only between him and all present, but also with all now living who will yet share the same impression; and, more than that, he feels the mysterious gladness of a communion which, reaching beyond the grave, unites us with all men of the past who have been moved by the same feelings and with all men of the future who will yet be touched by them. And this effect is produced both by religious art which transmits feelings of love of God and one's neighbor, and by universal art transmitting the very simplest feelings common to all men.

In *What Is Art?* with breath-taking execution and that maddening consistency which is as much the hallmark of pride as of humility, Tolstoy consigned to the category of bad art *War and Peace* and *Anna Karenina*, along with the rest of his fiction up to that point except for two small tales. Nor was he above indulging in some rather ponderous humor at the expense of Wagner's *Ring of the Nibelung* and the more opaque poetic effusions of the Decadents and Symbolists. Yet in organization and persuasive argumentation, and in the variety of examples drawn from literature and life, Tolstoy never surpassed this achievement in any of his controversial works. Though one may fairly accuse him at times of being whimsical and captious in his aesthetic views, they are never the expressions of a writer's vanity.

In one place in the book Tolstoy remarked that he knew his theory of art would be considered an irrational paradox at which one could only be amazed. Nor did he understate the case. Although George Bernard Shaw, with an aesthetic fissure in his brain as deep and wide as that of Tolstoy, hailed the work with delight, the majority of critics abroad quickly belabored it into an undeserved oblivion from which it has not been exhumed to this day. Perhaps their asperity may be pardoned in the face of Tolstoy's expressed sympathy for the truculent judgment of another author, namely, that "critics are the stupid who discuss the wise." It must be said that for the most part critics failed to come to grips with his altogether challenging definition of art and concentrated their shafts on his withering application of it to certain generally accepted great works of art. Apart from the examples, what deeply offended most foreign reviewers, perhaps because of garbled translations, was their belief that Tolstoy had elevated the simple peasant as a touchstone or criterion of all art. What he actually claimed for the peasant was what he claimed for every man, that is, if his capacity to share another's feelings had not been atrophied or perverted, he would be capable of responding to the art which *he* personally required.

Tolstoy was never satisfied with *What Is Art?* He felt it to be weak in various places, and he returned to the subject often in his diary and letters. There lurked in his mind a suspicion that something in the "mysterious and important" matter of art had not found its proper place in his aesthetic theory. However, anyone who regards art as not merely an amusement or a recreation, but one of culture's noblest achievements, will discover an enduring interest in Tolstoy's treatise. For its dominant emphasis, unlike that of many books on the subject, is precisely on the theme that the right practice of art in spreading the best feelings among men bears a direct relation to the whole life of humanity.

4

Though it is his major effort in the field, *What Is Art?* does not reflect the full measure of Tolstoy's preoccupation with aesthetics and literary criticism. Scattered through volumes of his diary, many letters, and memoirs of family and friends who quote his judgments is a substantial body of often acute observations on the theater, painting, music, sculpture, and on literature in particular. In addition he contributed introductions to the literary works of others and also wrote several critical articles on belles-lettres. Only the most significant items of this rich material can be discussed here.

There is a stubborn intellectual honesty in Tolstoy's appraisals of the works of famous Russian authors of his own lifetime, but his arbitrariness is frequently matched by penetrating insights. For example, he once told Chekhov that Gorky invented his psychology and wrote about feelings he had never experienced—a keen and just criticism of major failings in Gorky's fiction. But about Chekhov, whom Tolstoy deeply admired, he wrote: "Chekhov is an incomparable artist, an artist of life. And the merit of his creative work is that he is understood and accepted not only by every Russian, but by all humanity."

Of all Chekhov's numerous short stories, "The Darling" appears to have been Tolstoy's favorite. Gorky recalls him speaking of it with rapture to a group of listeners who included Chekhov: "It is like lace," he said, "made by a chaste young girl, there were such lacemakers in olden times who used to depict all their lives, all their dreams of happiness in the pattern. They dreamed in designs of all that was dear to them, wove all their pure, uncertain love into their lace."

In fact, Tolstoy wrote a brief article (1905) on "The Darling," in which he maintained that Chekhov, in the characterization of the heroine, intended to satirize the "new woman of the day, a seeker after equality with men." But, Tolstoy explains, the god of poetry in Chekhov forbade him to ridicule her "and commanded him to bless, and he blessed, and involuntarily clothed that sweet creature in such a wonderful radiance that she will always remain a type of what woman can be in order to be happy herself and to cause the happiness of those with whom her fate is united. This story is excellent because its effect is unintentional."

Chekhov would have been more amused than irritated if he could have read this gratuitous criticism—it was not published until after his death. He was not poking fun at the "new woman" in "The Darling," and the poetical effect which Tolstoy admired was in no sense unintentional but a conscious achievement of his art. Tolstoy's failure, as here, to plumb the depths of Chekhov's tenderness and charity for those who suffered because of man's inhumanity is also reflected in his comment on Chekhov's "Attack of Nerves," the hero of which, Tolstoy remarked, ought first to have slept with one of the prostitutes before experiencing the anguish of a guilty conscience.

Though Tolstoy's preference for Chekhov's brief early stories, where a simple theme is directly treated with strong emphasis on moral feeling, reflects the aesthetic standards of *What Is Art?*, he was nevertheless one of the very few during Chekhov's lifetime to perceive that he was much less an imitator of anything than a brilliant innovator who initiated a new development in Russian literature. Tolstoy pointed out once that "as an artist Chekhov cannot even be compared with the old Russian writers—Turgenev, Dostoevsky, or myself. Chekhov has his own manner, like the Impressionists. You see a man daubing on whatever paint happens to be near at hand, apparently without selection, and it seems as though these paints bear no relation to one another. But if you step back a certain distance and look again, you will get a complete, over-all impression. Before you there is a vivid, unchallengeable picture of nature." Tolstoy grasped, as few did then, that Chekhov's choice of the short story was a conscious effort to avoid traditional, introductory, biographical build-ups and lengthy descriptions, just as avoidance of detailed linear emphasis was intended to regenerate everyday realism in an impressionistic manner, in order to present a real and not a conventionalized picture of life.

On the whole, Tolstoy, who translated two of Maupassant's tales, favored him over Chekhov as a short-story writer, because—he thought—the Frenchman distilled greater joy out of life. But Chekhov, he said, "is cleaner than Maupassant. The illusion of truth in Chekhov is complete, his pieces produce the impression of a stereoscope." In fact, Tolstoy severely criticized Maupassant's novels in a lengthy article, "Introduction to the Works of Guy de Maupassant" (1894), which launched the second volume of his writings in Russian translation. On first acquaintance with Maupassant's fiction, he praised him as one of the best writers of the age, because—he said—he perfectly understood and valued the negative side of the relations of the sexes as no other writer had done. In the course of working on the article, however, he grew disillusioned with this aspect of Maupassant's fiction. He wrote to his son Leo: "I am working on the introduction to Maupassant. The wretches have announced that whoever buys the second volume of Maupassant will have Tolstoy's article on Maupassant, and now I must present the article or be scolded. But Maupassant's moral filth has become repugnant to me, and I have thrown away my first introduction and begun to write a new one, in which I wish to say what I think about art, but as yet I have not been able to express it."

The article is a brilliant example of Tolstoy's analytical method in literary criticism but is flawed by his excessive demand for moral content in a work of art. He saw reflected in Maupassant's novels the desire to achieve a cheap *réclame* by concentrating on the pleasure of sexual love, a subject popular in the literature of bourgeois circles. "In all his novels after *Bel-Ami*," Tolstoy wrote, "Maupassant evidently submitted to the theory which ruled not only in his circle in Paris, but which now rules everywhere among artists: that for a work of art it is not only unnecessary to have a clear conception of what is right and wrong, but that on the contrary an artist should completely ignore all moral questions, there being a certain artistic merit in so doing."

On the other hand, in the best of Maupassant's short stories, Tolstoy argues, he wrote about what touched or revolted his moral feelings. "And it is in this that the wonderful quality of every true artist lives. . . . His talent teaches its possessor and leads him forward along the path of moral development, compelling him to love what deserves love and to hate what deserves hate. An artist is an artist because he sees things not as he wishes to see them but as they really are." In short, what he is saying in the article is that Maupassant at times betrays his genius, writing about some worthless Paris seducer with greater love than he feels for his victims, but in the end he cannot help detecting what is good, and it forces him against his will on to the path of truth. That is, vision reveals truth to the real artist, which compels him to face fundamental moral questions that lead to regeneration, the proper function of art.

Though Tolstoy's perverse opinions on Shakespeare are commonly attributed to the intellectual rigidity that took possession of him after his religious conversion, his "dissidence of dissent," as it were, in all matters intellectual and critical was a characteristic trait of his nature from his youth. In literary no less than in political, social, and religious questions, he seemed to strive always for originality in discussion or writing. As early as 1856 the editor Panaev said to a friend who called on him just as Tolstoy left: "How sorry I am that you are late. What marvels you would have heard! You would have learned that Shakespeare is an ordinary writer, and that our astonishment and delight over Shakespeare are nothing more than a desire to keep up with others and the habit of repeating foreign opinions."

Forty years later, in *Shakespeare and the Drama* (1906), a lengthy article that takes on the proportions of a small book, Tolstoy feeds fat the ancient grudge he had for the Bard of Avon, for his dislike had been intensified by the new demands he made upon literature in terms of feeling, infectiousness, form, philosophical outlook, and morality. After declaring that he had always experienced feelings of repulsion, weariness, and bewilderment on reading Shakespeare's plays, "Now," he says "before writing this article, as an old man of seventy-five [he began the work in 1903], wishing once more to check my conclusions, I have again read the whole of Shakespeare . . . and have experienced the same feelings still more strongly, no longer with perplexity but with a firm and unshakable conviction that the undisputed fame Shakespeare enjoys as a great genius—which makes writers of our time imitate him, and readers and spectators, distorting their aesthetic and ethical sense, seek nonexistent qualities in him—is a great evil, as every falsehood is." He then frankly anticipates that the majority of people will not even admit the possibility of his views being correct, but he firmly asserts that he will try as best he can "to show why I think Shakespeare cannot be admitted to be either a writer of great genius or even an average one."

To prove his point, Tolstoy elected, with perhaps some malice prepense, to make a detailed analysis of *King Lear*, a play which is placed by some Shakespearean scholars today at the very summit of his art. But Tolstoy demonstrates to his own satisfaction that *King Lear* does not fulfil the most elementary and generally recognized demands of art; that the characters speak not a language of their own, but an unnatural, affected Shakespearean language which no real people could ever have spoken anywhere; that the play lacks a sense of proportion; that its contents reflect a vulgar view of life which regards the elevation of the great ones of the earth as a genuine superiority while despising the comman man and repudiating not only religious, but even any humanitarian efforts directed toward the alteration of the existing order of society; and, finally, that the play lacks sincerity. Generalizing on these "faults," Tolstoy finds them present to some extent in most of Shakespeare's plays.

He argues that "If there is a difference in the speech of Shakespeare's characters, it is only that Shakespeare makes different speeches for his characters, and not that they speak differently." And the plays, in general, are devoid of a sense of proportion, without which, he asserts, "there never was or could be an artist, just as without a sense of rhythm there cannot be a musician." The trouble with those who try to make the praise of Shakespeare convincing, Tolstoy affirms, is that they have composed an aesthetic theory, "according to which a definite religious view is not at all necessary for the creation of works of art in general or for the drama in particular; that for the inner content of a play it is quite enough to depict passions and human characters; that not only is no religious illumination of the matter presented required, but that art ought to be objective, that is to say, it should depict occurrences quite independently of any valuation of what is good or bad."

It appears that Tolstoy did not intend to publish *Shakespeare and the Drama* during his lifetime and that he did so in 1906 only upon the urging of his chief disciple, V. G. Chertkov. Its appearance in English translation resulted in an interesting exchange of letters between him and George Bernard Shaw, who was an admirer of Tolstoy and who agreed with his condemnation of certain social and religious evils and with his conviction that civilization would not improve without a moral and intellectual change in man. Although they differed on the means of bringing about this change, it is not surprising that both men, in some few respects, had reached the same position on Shakespeare. When Chertkov was translating *Shakespeare and the Drama* in England, he wrote Shaw for advice on some points and also gave him a general idea of the conclusions of the work. Shaw replied, enthusiastically embracing Tolstoy's views as Chertkov described them. He agreed that Shakespeare possessed no real philosophy of life, and that his plays revealed no religious, moral, or social thought worthy of consideration. "After the criticism of Tolstoy," he wrote, "Shakespeare as a *thinker* must be discarded, for under the scrutiny of such a gigantic, bold critic and realist as Tolstoy, he will in no sense pass the test."

Encouraged by Shaw's attitude, Chertkov finally sent him the complete translation. Upon reading it, Shaw at once realized that he had far overshot the mark in identifying himself with Tolstoy's views on Shakespeare. He hastened to write Chertkov a long letter, soon followed by another, which contained a sharp criticism of *Shakespeare and the Drama* and, in passing, some of Shaw's best observations on Shakespeare and his plays. Unlike Tolstoy, Shaw made a sharp distinction between Shakespeare the thinker and Shakespeare the artist. He could go along with Tolstoy in dismissing Shakespeare the thinker as inconsequential, but as an artist, he stoutly maintained, Shakespeare was irresistible. In one of the letters, Shaw wrote that in his own criticism of the dramatist "he had endeavored in no small degree to open the eyes of Englishmen to the emptiness of Shakespeare's philosophy, to the superficiality and unoriginality of his moral views, to his weakness and confusion as a thinker, to his snobbery, to his vulgar prejudices, to his ignorance, to every aspect of his undeserved reputation as a great philosopher." But, he continued, "No one would listen to me if I took it into my head to support my protest by denying his humor, his gaiety, his capactiy to create characters more real for us than actual living people, his tenderness, but chiefly his unusual power as a musician of words." The trouble, Shaw concluded, was that Tolstoy attempted to judge Shakespeare from the point of view of abstract logic. "Life is not logical," he cautioned, "and it is not for Tolstoy, writing his productions as a poet, to condemn Shakespeare for not writing his as a jurist." In the end, Shaw allowed that Tolstoy's position on Shakespeare was to a certain extent a healthy one, but that the work as a whole was very bad.

Lovers of Shakespeare might justly call down a plague on both these detractors, but the distinctions that Shaw draws on behalf of Tolstoy are at least arguable by the unprejudiced. That Tolstoy, especially in his later years, often assumed a wrong-headed, indefensible posture on questions of art and literary criticism is demonstrable. Yet with this stricture in mind, there is little he wrote on these subjects that fails to repay the efforts of the curious and objective reader. The position is well summed up by the eminent Shakespearean scholar, Professor G. Wilson Knight, in his article "Shakespeare and Tolstoy." There he describes Tolstoy's writings on art as "a massive collection of some of the most masculine, incisive, and important criticism that exists; all, whether we agree or disagree, of so rock-like an integrity and simplicity that its effect is invariably tonic and invigorating, and often points us directly, as in this essay on Shakespeare, to facts before unobserved, yet both obvious and extremely significant."

VIII

LATER SHORT STORIES

I

After his first two major full-length novels, *War and Peace* and *Anna Karenina*, Tolstoy did not neglect the short story form which had played so prominent a part in his youthful literary endeavors. In any comparison of his accomplishments in this genre during the early and later periods, one is struck by the somewhat limited output in the second in terms of the forty years involved. Several reasons for the disparity come to mind, but perhaps the important one is that Tolstoy's enormous success in the novel served to lessen his interest in the short story.

Still more striking is the marked thematic difference between the short stories in the two periods. With a few exceptions those in the later period do not appear to have been written to enhance a literary reputation. Most of them seem to be inspired by an uneasy conscience or a deliberate subjective purpose, yet among them are several short stories that have often been acclaimed as Tolstoy's greatest. Of course, the difference in his approach and subject matter was connected with the spiritual crisis he underwent at the beginning of the 1880's, an experience which, as already indicated, altered the course of his life as well as his attitude toward art.

The earliest group of these short stories, written in 1872 between *War and Peace* and *Anna Karenina*, Tolstoy regarded as "Tales for Children." He was dubious about the practice of writing stories specifically for youngsters and would probably have agreed with Chekhov's advice that one should select for children something truly artistic that has been written for adults. The tales in this group appear to be closely connected with Tolstoy's return to pedagogical pursuits in 1870, one result of which, as we have seen, was his *ABC Book* containing a complete educational curriculum for beginning pupils. In preparing its reading selections, he pored over collections of Russian mediaeval legends and the folk tales of a dozen countries, paying particular attention to the style of those he translated. The simplicity and clarity of these folk narratives plainly influenced the original tales he wrote for his *ABC Book*. In fact, more than ten years before he began to think seriously about the ideas that guided his notable treatise, *What Is Art?*, he had hit upon one of its salient contentions—that the language of sophisticated literature was less effective, artistically, than the language of the so-called popular literature of uneducated folk.

There is much of the fetching artlessness of folk tales in "God Sees the Truth, but Waits," for the emotional power of its message of forgiveness gains in impressiveness by virtue of the uncontrived simplicity of motivation and characterization. In the end, Aksyonov's triumphant faith in God transforms an unjust punishment into an act of beatification. The theme of a merchant who was condemned for a crime he did not commit and who accepted his tribulations in a spirit of Christian forgiveness was a favorite of Tolstoy's, and he used it earlier, in memorable circumstances, in the story told in *War and Peace* by the peasant, Platon Karataev.

Though a youngster might not easily perceive the moral significance of "God Sees the Truth, but Waits," he would have no difficulty appreciating the simple feelings of fear, courage, pity, and endurance which Tolstoy illustrated without didacticism in "A Prisoner in the Caucasus." Moreover, the youngster would understand and approve the efforts of Dina, the charmingly portrayed little Tartar girl, to free the Russian officer Zhilin, captured by her people, even though she risked severe punishment. She was won over not so much by the clever toys he made for her as by his courage, fearlessness, and strength of character, which aroused in her feminine feelings strange in one so young. The adult reader, however, will take pleasure in the work as a well-told story of adventure in the tradition of Tolstoy's early Caucasian tales, but at the same time differing from them in its special individuality and in its clarity and sincerity of expression. And again, like the early Caucasian short stories, it is based on a personal experience— once, in an exposed position as a cadet in the Russian forces, Tolstoy barely escaped capture by the Tartars.

The third and last story in this group for children, "The Bear-Hunt," likewise grew out of an actual incident—in 1858 Tolstoy, while hunting with a friend, was attacked by a huge bear that had been wounded, and he almost lost his life. Though the details of the real and fictional accounts are quite similar, in the latter one may observe the transmuting power of Tolstoy's art manifesting itself in the wonderfully realistic descriptions of winter scenes on the first day of the hunt, the sleeping and awakening in the woods, and much else, all of which appears to be entirely imaginary.

It is worth pointing out that Tolstoy regarded "God Sees the Truth, but Waits" and "A Prisoner in the Caucasus" as the

best of all his many short stories. In consigning the whole
corpus of his works to the category of "bad art" in *What Is
Art?* he made exceptions of these two tales, placing the first in
the highest category of "religious art" and the second in the
category of "universal art."

2

It has been pointed out that after his spiritual conversion
Tolstoy devoted himself to the theory and practice of a new
faith that amounted to a form of Christian anarchism incompatible with the kind of emphasis he had been placing on
fiction. There is even a suggestion that he would like to have
broken cleanly with art just as he flatly rejected the kind of life
he had previously led. If now, however, he was unable to
abandon imaginative writing, he was determined that it would
be consistent with the new morality and ethics to which he
subscribed. And it must be said that nearly everything he did
write after his conversion was conceived and executed, in
varying degrees, in the spirit of his new faith. That is, he
sought to create in terms of the categories he established in
What Is Art?—religious art that transmits feelings of love of
God and one's neighbor, and universal art that transmits the
very simplest feelings common to all men. The remarkable fact
is that not a few of these works must be included among his
most memorable artistic achievements.

The qualities Tolstoy now sought in art he detected in the
old religious legends and folk tales he had combed in connection with the compilation of his *ABC Book*. The fact that the
Russian masses lacked easy accessibility to inexpensive editions
of such literature prompted him to explore the matter. One
consequence was the establishment, in 1884, of a publishing
firm called *Intermediary*, the main purpose of which was to
make available to the people cheap booklets containing fiction
and illustrations reflecting the essence of Tolstoy's Christian

teaching. Initially the business was headed by his disciple V. G. Chertkov.

In 1882 Tolstoy had published "What Men Live By," a beautiful retelling of the old legend of the angle sent to earth by God to teach men to live by love. Chertkov, impressed by the widespread popularity of this short story, urged Tolstoy to contribute similar tales to *Intermediary*. He did, and no doubt the initial popularity of the firm's booklets may be attributed to the fact that three of the early ones contained stories from his pen. His conviction that the masses would read good literature if they could afford to buy it was proved to the hilt, for these *Intermediary* booklets, Russia's "paperbacks," priced at the equivalent of a cent, sold twelve million copies in the first four years of the existence of the firm.

The second grouping among these later short stories could be described as "Folk Tales and Legends." It is made up of a series of narratives written mostly for *Intermediary* and hence aimed primarily at peasants and workers, but their simplicity and charm delight young and old of all social classes. Sources of most if not all of these stories may be found in oral and written literature of the folk, but in retelling the tales Tolstoy has made them entirely his own. He declared in an article, "Truth in Art" (1887), that "there are fairy tales, parables, legends, in which marvellous things are described that never happened or ever could happen, and these legends, fairy tales, and fables are true, because they show wherein the will of God has always been, and is, and will be: they show the truth of the kingdom of God."

In these pieces for *Intermediary* he strove to retain the artlessness of folk literature, its customary trappings of devils, imps, supernatural happenings, repetition of motifs, and other-worldly plots, but at the same time he used them to impart his own moral and religious convictions. And the narrative style he employs has nothing of the saturated realism of his previous fiction. It has the biblical simplicity of one of his favorite tales, that of Joseph and his coat of many colors. The unknown author of this story, Tolstoy writes in *What Is Art?*" did not need to describe in detail, as would be done nowadays, the blood-stained coat of Joseph, the dwelling and dress of Jacob, the pose and attire of Potiphar's wife, and how adjusting the bracelet on her left arm she said, 'Come to me,' and so on, because the content of feeling in this tale is so strong that all details except the most essential—such as that Joseph went out into another room to weep—are superfluous and would only hinder the transmission of emotion. And therefore this tale is accessible to all men, touches people of all nations and classes young and old, and has lasted to our times and will last for thousands of years to come."

"Two Old Men" (1885), "Where Love Is, God Is" (1885), and "The Repentant Sinner" (1886) fall into Tolstoy's category of "religious art" which transmits feelings of love of God and one's neighbor. The moral of the first story—that the best way to keep one's vow to God and to do His will is for each man to show love and do good to others—does not seem contrived in this appealing narrative of the two old friends who set out on a pilgrimage to Jerusalem. One fails to get there because of his compulsion to help a starving family on the road, whereas his comrade, who reaches the goal and performs all the conventional acts of worship, comes away religiously unmoved. The bland flavor of biblical narrative suffuses "Where Love Is, God Is," and the same may be said of "The Repentant Sinner," but the "instructional" purpose of both stories is allowed to remain too close to the surface.

Characteristic folk-tale content and narrative method predominate in the remaining stories of the group, except for the very brief pieces, "Evil Allures, but God Endures" (1885), "Little Girls Wiser than Men" (1885), and "Elias" (1885), which Tolstoy wrote as illustrative texts to accompany pictures reproduced in *Intermediary*. His intention is to portray the simplest feelings common to all men which, as indicated, he later associated with the category, "universal art." In this respect he succeeds, sometimes quite brilliantly. However, in pure folk literature a moral lesson, if any, is never made explicit, and whenever present it is subordinated to narrative interest in incident and character. This is not always the case with Tolstoy. Though the story of the enmity of peasant neighbors in "A Spark Neglected Burns the House" (1885) is absorbing, the old father's moral preaching conveys the impression that the incidents were deliberately devised to prove that one must forgive one's enemies and, if necessary, turn the other cheek.

On the other hand, "The Story of Ivan the Fool" (1885) is an unblemished folk tale, in which Ivan emerges as a convincing popular hero. There is some humor in Ivan's repeated frustration of the devil's designs on him, and in his dedication to hard work there is an exemplification of a solid folk virtue which is contrasted with the vain hopes of easy success on the part of his two brothers. It has been said that the story contains an indictment of militarism and commercialism, but if this is so the indictment is never allowed to obtrude upon the artistic unity of the narrative. The same may be said of the so-called anti-war element in "The Empty Drum" (1891), another effective retelling of a folk tale which, according to Tolstoy, was still current in the Volga region. There is also humor in "The Three Hermits" (1886). The rather pompous bishop, after teaching the Lord's Prayer to the ignorant hermits on an island, decides they need no further lessons in the faith when he discovers them running on the surface of the water in pursuit of his ship to seek further instruction from him.

The moral lesson in "The Imp and the Crust" (1886) is a natural part of the story, in which the devil finally tricks the kind peasant into drunkenness. If Tolstoy's handling of this gem of a folk tale is regarded as a plea for temperance, it is a conclusion that must be drawn by the reader, for it is never explicitly stated in the text. Tolstoy's dramatization of the story, a comedy entitled *The First Distiller* (1886), which will be considered in a later chapter, does turn out to be an amusing piece of forthright temperance propaganda.

Though interesting characteristics of the Russian peasantry are reflected in "A Grain As Big As a Hen's Egg" (1886) and "The Godson" (1886), the first appears to have been written specifically to demonstrate that people then, unlike their forebears, have ceased to live by their own labor and depend on that of others. The second is oddly complicated for a story in the folk-tale tradition, perhaps because Tolstoy imposed upon it the dual purpose of showing that one must care more about others than about oneself, and that one must not fear death if one wishes to make one's heart fast to God. It is unnecessary to append a moral to the well-known and consummately narrated "How Much Land Does a Man Need?" (1886), for the whole story is about the traditional greed of the peasants for land. The failing betrays one of them, who in the end discovers too late that all the land he requires is the six feet in which he is buried. This uncompromising object lesson in the vanity of human wishes was later repudiated by Chekhov in his tale "Gooseberries," where the narrator pointedly declares: "Man needs not six feet of earth, not a farm, but the whole globe, all nature, where he will have room for the full play of all the capacities and peculiarities of his free spirit."

Before the end of the 1880's Tolstoy appears to have lost interest in turning popular legends and tales into short stories that would illuminate his religious and moral convictions. In 1903, however, a special circumstance led him to attempt more stories of this kind. He was invited to contribute to a volume on behalf of persecuted Jews of Russia, especially those attacked that year in the terrible pogroms at Kishinev. Other distinguished authors, including Chekhov, gladly offered manuscripts for the proposed book. Tolstoy's three brief stories for this purpose were translated into Yiddish by the eminent Jewish writer Sholom Aleichem and appeared in a volume published in Warsaw.

The economy of means in the first of these stories "Esarhaddon, King of Assyria," with its simple moral preachment that when you harm others you harm yourself because all life is one, is matched by "Work, Death, and Sickness," a retelling, says Tolstoy, of a religious legend current among South American Indians. Here, in four short pages, he drives home the lesson that work ought to unite all men so that they might live in unity and love. The last of these tales written to aid the Jewish sufferers, "Three Questions," is equally succinct in detailing the manner in which a baffled king discovers answers to his problems.

3

The final group, his last short stories, consists of four which Tolstoy never published in his lifetime. In them he reverts to his early manner of fiction-writing before his spiritual conversion, with the difference that he still remains influenced by the special concerns of his new faith. At times he draws upon personal experiences as he did in so many of his previous creative works. This is especially true of "Memoirs of a Madman," which he began to write as early as 1884 and apparently never finished to his own satisfaction. It is a rather thinly disguised fictionized treatment of the oppressive fear of death, which he experienced before his religious change, and its relation to his growing belief that the kind of life he led then was irrational, fit only for a madman, and must be abandoned. Scenes of the visitation of death are as intensely and brilliantly realized as Prince Andrew's striking encounter with death in *War and Peace*.

In "After the Ball" (1903), the seventy-five-year-old Tolstoy goes back for inspiration to a love affair as a youthful
student at Kazan University. But how vividly and freshly he
evokes the atmosphere of the past by employing the saturated
realism and psychological probing of his earlier art! At the end
of the story, however, there lurks the aged Tolstoy's implied
condemnation of the state as a kind of conspiracy not only to
exploit citizens, but to demoralize them as well. For after the
ball, when the young Ivan Vasilyevich, his mind still filled
with the ecstasy of love, accidentally witnesses the horrifying
spectacle of a deserter being fatally clubbed through the
gauntlet of his fellow-soldiers at the command of a colonel,
who is his beloved's father, the hero's passion for the daughter
not only grows cold, but he mentally vows never to enter any
form of government service.

There can be no doubt that "Fedor Kuzmich" (1905) was
intended to be a long narrative, but even in its present unfinished state it may stand as a rather well-rounded short story.
Again Tolstoy returns to artistic memories and methods of an
earlier period, specifically to the historical novel, *War and
Peace*, and one of its principal characters—Alexander I.
Though there seems to be no diminution in his skill in handling
the material of historical fiction, it is also clear that Alexander's
attraction for him now is based more on ideological than
artistic considerations. Accepting the allegation, believed by
many at the time, that Alexander falsified his death in 1825 and
secretly disappeared and became a repentant and holy hermit
in Siberia, Tolstoy undertook to portray him in this light. Obviously he was intrigued by the analogy between his own
hopes and aspirations in his last years and those of this emperor,
who supposedly turned his back on a worldly existence in
order, in poverty and humility, to live a religious life of
thought and good deeds.

In the few highly concentrated pages devoted to "Alyosha"

(1905), one of the last short stories Tolstoy wrote, he is again the pure artist, untroubled and uninfluenced by moral or religious preachments. Or perhaps it would be better to say that all he believed and hoped for is artistically sublimated in the radiant image of "Alyosha the pot," the simple peasant drudge who in his cheerful, self-sacrificing service to others discovers that perfect peace which Tolstoy sought for in vain at the end of his life. The story is a perfect masterpiece in miniature.

IX

LATER SHORT NOVELS

I

In addition to the short story, Tolstoy also devoted a substantial amount of creative effort, after *War and Peace* and *Anna Karenina*, to that longer type of fiction which he had attempted in his earlier period—the short novel. Though they vary a great deal in length, no one of them could properly be regarded as either a short story or a novel. For like the earlier short novels, each involves a number of characters and a frame of reference too extensive for the concentrated focus of the short story but not extensive enough for the expansive structure of the full-length novel. Among these eight remaining short novels are several of his most remarkable creations in fiction.

An objective approach to the human condition may be discerned in the early short novels, but in the later ones Tolstoy's own moral presence, combined with a subjective spiritual element, is frequently felt, although he is careful, in the best of them, to embody his personal views in impeccable artistic form. The different emphasis is largely a consequence of Tolstoy's sharply altered outlook on life—all the later short novels were written after his searing spiritual experience of 1880–81. During these remaining years the art of fiction, with some few exceptions, became a medium for conveying his search for truth and for urging individual self-perfection, opposition to violence in any form, and man's duty to live by the moral law. Even certain of the ascetic rules of his new faith, which he tried to live up to, find reflection in his tales—the need to abandon private property, to achieve self-sufficiency through physical labor in the matter of one's essential wants, to be chaste, and to subscribe to vegetarianism and abstinence from liquor and tobacco.

However sincere was Tolstoy's reluctance to practice his art after his spiritual conversion, he could never get himself to deny an instinct that was central to his being. If the elaborate theory of artistic creation in *What Is Art?* was in essence an aesthetic expression of his new philosophy, designed in part to justify the future fiction he felt an inner compulsion to write, the results frequently indicate that the literary artist in him transcended the moral and religious preacher. For despite the mass of religious, philosophical, and moral books and articles he wrote during this last period, he produced a surprising body of belles-lettres. And much more fiction might have been turned out if it had not been for a special circumstance. In 1891 Tolstoy publicly renounced the copyrights of all he had written after 1881, the time of his spiritual conversion. This decision became one of the principal reasons for the prolonged and tragic struggle that developed between him and his wife, who had taken upon herself the publication of his works. Every new artistic effort of her husband could cause a renewal of the family quarrel, for she invariably pleaded for the right of first publication for the sake of financial gain, the very thing he was trying to avoid. This unhappy situation made him hesitate to write fiction at all. Some stories that he began he failed to complete for years, and if finished, he would conceal them from his wife or hold up their publication for a long time. Several of his finest tales did not appear until the posthumous edition of his unpublished works in 1911. It is reasonably certain that he avoided finishing several stories and one play because of his reluctance to add to the quarrels with his wife over publication rights.

This situation makes it extremely difficult to date exactly the writing of some of his later short novels, especially those Tolstoy worked on for several years or kept hidden from his wife. And since four of the eight tales were first printed posthumously, publication dates have no certain relation to actual composition. Therefore it seems best to consider these stories chronologically according to the year or years in which they were written, and when that data is not accurately ascertainable, according to the year in which Tolstoy finished the writing of each story, dates which are available in every case.

If in several of the short novels under consideration Tolstoy attempts, as a supreme rationalist, to identify the principle of life with reason, it is the irrational human conscience that brings about the conversion of his heroes through experiences essentially mystical in nature. Though in such narratives Tolstoy is usually concerned with bringing the actions and thoughts of his characters into harmony with his new beliefs, he rarely ceases to be the literary artist in matters of language, form, and content.

The fear of death, a problem with which Tolstoy had long been preoccupied, lies behind the mystical experiences of the main characters in *The Death of Ivan Ilych* (finished 1886; published 1886) and *Master and Man* (finished 1895; published 1895), two of his greatest masterpieces in the genre of the short novel. The public hailed *The Death of Ivan Ilych*, for it was the first substantial artistic work that he had written since *Anna Karenina* nine years before. At last it seemed that the celebrated author had returned to the art that had won him international fame.

This short novel, which is an account of the spiritual conversion of a judge, an ordinary, unthinking, vulgar man, in the face of the terrible fear of approaching death, is a problem story in which Tolstoy does not so much preach as communicate experience. In it he not only reverts to the wonderful realism of his early fiction, but adds an emphasis new and startling in the development of Russian literature. Although Gorky is often credited with freeing nineteenth-century Russian realism from its genteel tradition of inoffensiveness, a tradition not unlike that of English Victorian fiction, Tolstoy preceded him in this respect in *The Death of Ivan Ilych*, where he dwells with unsparing detail on the physical horrors of disease and death. But the story is also filled with those psychologically realistic and perceptive touches made familiar to us by earlier novels—Peter Ivanovich's efforts, at a solemn moment, to suppress the rebellious metal springs of the pouf on which he sits at Ivan Ilych's funeral; the subtle indications of the mourners' insincerity, suggested by their concentration on unrelated trivia; the indirect hints of the dissimulation and hypocrisy of Ivan Ilych's grieving wife and colleagues, who barely disguise their secret concern over the advantages or disadvantages that will accrue to them because of his death. Yet we somehow know that Ivan Ilych would have behaved in similar fashion in the event of the decease of his wife or of one of his partners in the law.

Ivan Ilych's life, remarks Tolstoy, had been most simple and ordinary and therefore most terrible. He is very strict in the fulfillment of his legal duties, and he considers his duty to be what is so considered by those in authority. As a magistrate, he particularly enjoys power, and in his examinations of those on trial, his main concern is to eliminate all considerations irrelevant to the legal aspects of the case, in short, to eliminate every vestige of human sympathy or pity. His heartlessness is neatly and ironically revealed during his illness, when he hopefully asks the examining physician: "We sick people probably often put inappropriate questions. But tell me, in general, is this complaint dangerous, or not?' The doctor looked at him sternly over his spectacles with one eye, as if to say: 'Prisoner, if you will not keep to the questions put to you, I shall be obliged to have you removed from the court.' "

During his long wasting illness, Ivan Ilych tries at times to justify his life which he always imagined had been a good one. But when he feels the end approaching, in mortal despair he realizes that he has been living a lie and indulging in utter self-deception. These clarifying moments come to him with particular poignancy upon beholding the sincere grief of his young son over his sufferings and when he submits to the cheerful, self-sacrificing ministrations of his simple peasant servant Gerasim. He had discovered sympathy and pity where he had never expected to find them. Thus prepared, shortly before his death an inner light mystically illumines the clouded understanding of Ivan Ilych. He suddenly perceives that man's essential life belongs to the spirit, a realm of feeling where well-being is achieved in the loving community of people. In truth, death for Ivan Ilych ultimately becomes an awakening. He asks forgiveness of his family for his sins and welcomes death, transported by the inner light of faith, renunciation, and love.

In *Master and Man* the same theme is treated with equal effectiveness in a totally different setting of peasants and merchants, and the story is told in a style that falls between Tolstoy's earlier method of saturated realism and his post-conversion manner of simple unadorned narrative designed to appeal to the mass reader. Here and elsewhere we sense that his aim is to relate facts with as much warmth and persuasiveness as possible and hence the prose he creates is magnificent. It has been said that whenever he wrote a sentence which seemed too elegant, he hastened to disarrange it so that it did not appear to be polished. He appreciated only what was left after he had rejected all conventions and only what could live without artifice. When obliged to choose, he always preferred rudimentary expressions to the most ingenious and refined. There is no grandeur, he remarked in *War and Peace*, where there is no simplicity, no truth. And his immediate followers in Russian fiction, such as Chekhov, Gorky, and Bunin, strove to avoid what might be described as a polished style.

When Tolstoy finished *Master and Man*, he sent the manuscript to a close friend whose critical judgment he valued, with the comment: "It is so long since I've written anything artistic that I truly do not know whether it ought to be printed. I wrote it with great satisfaction. . . ." Actually, Tolstoy feared, at the age of sixty-seven, that his creative powers were slipping, and the prompt response of his friend: "My God! how splendid, priceless it is . . ." quite reassured him.

Extensive concentration on the blizzard in *Master and Man* recalls the famous description in "The Snow Storm," a short story written almost forty years earlier, but it must be said that the effort of his old age is in no sense artistically inferior to that of his youth. "The Snow Storm" is centered almost exclusively on closely observed nature and incident. In *Master and Man*, nature is employed as the background of a profound story that emerges from Tolstoy's feelings and from his mature understanding of life and death, and the sustained beauty of the construction ennobles its great theme.

The merchant Vasily's relentless ambition to accumulate money is contrasted with the harsh lot of his kindly peasant worker, Nikita, whose existence of endless toil and service is hardly sweetened by the knowledge that his master regularly cheats him. The contrast tragically deepens when master and man are threatened with freezing to death as they lose their way at night in a raging blizzard—Vasily had insisted on braving the storm in his sleigh in order to anticipate competitors in the sale of a woodlot. Finally, hopelessly marooned in the bitter cold and swirling snow, they can go no further. Nikita wraps himself up in his threadbare coat and waits. Death does not particularly worry him. In dying, he thinks, he will be in God's power and will not be ill-used by Him. It is a pity to give up what one is accustomed to, he tells himself, but he will get used to new things.

Meanwhile, the warmly clad master, worrying about missing out on the woodlot deal and thinking only of his growing fortune, mounts the unharnessed horse in an attempt to go on alone. But in the darkness and the storm he travels in a circle and comes back to the sleigh. Nikita, slowly freezing, begs him to give the money owing to him to his son and then asks his master's forgiveness. At this point the master, as in the case of the hero of *The Death of Ivan Ilych*, experiences an inner spiritual illumination. He lies on the body of his worker, wrapping around him the flaps of his huge fur coat. And as the warmth gradually revives Nikita, the master finds inexpressible joy and contentment in discovering the true life of brotherly contact with a fellow man. The next morning, when peasants dig them out of the snow, the worker is alive and the master dead.

The merchant's mystical experience at the end that brings about the victory of unselfishness over death seems entirely genuine and convincing. *Master and Man* embodies Tolstoy's ideal of religious art that has a universal appeal more successfully than other tales which he expressly designed for this purpose. Here truth is achieved by spiritual conviction rather than by the intellectual conviction that brings about the conversion of Tolstoy's hero in his novel *Resurrection*—a patent artistic error.

2

During the last half of his life Tolstoy was much concerned with sexual problems, both in terms of his personal behavior and as they related to certain tenets of his new faith. His diary reveals that before his marriage he indulged in the loose living not uncommon among young men of the gentry class. After his marriage, though not immune to extramarital temptations of the flesh, he appears to have been faithful to his wife. In his later years, however, he looked back with disgust and a guilty conscience on the excesses of his youth, and because of the moral demands of his new beliefs he grew deeply troubled over what he regarded as the sexual immorality of society. These concerns inspired two of his most powerful short novels, *The Devil* (written 1889; published posthumously 1911) and *The Kreutzer Sonata* (finished 1889; published 1891), sometimes referred to as his "sexual stories." Each has an autobiographical basis which is particularly in evidence in *The Devil*.

Shortly before his marriage in 1862 to a girl barely half his age, Tolstoy, with that incredible integrity so characteristic of him, allowed her to read his diary. There she found entries, among others of a similar nature, of his relations with a young married peasant woman, Aksinya, who lived in his village of Yasnaya Polyana. One entry reads: "Today, in the big old wood, I'm a fool, a brute. Her bronzed flush and her eyes. . . . I'm in love as never before in my life." Tolstoy admits in the diary that his feeling for Aksinya, by whom he had a son, was like that of a husband. Though he struggled against this passion, entries about Aksinya continue up to two years before his marriage, at which time he broke off the liaison. Tormented by her knowledge of this affair, his wife, in fits of jealous anger, more than once berated him. In fact, Aksinya, like Stepanida in *The Devil*, was by chance among several villagers who were once employed to clean in the Tolstoy household, and a servant pointed her out to the young wife as "that woman."

In *The Devil*, the passionate love affair of Irtenev and Stepanida, a young married peasant woman on his estate, duplicates the relations between Tolstoy and Aksinya, so closely indeed that Tolstoy felt it wise to conceal the manuscript from his wife. Though the ultimate consequences of Irtenev's guilty passion go beyond the Aksinya-Tolstoy relationship, these also have a curious autobiographical foundation. Marriage fails to quell Irtenev's illicit desires, and in a desperate effort to protect himself he confesses the affair to his uncle and asks him to accompany him on walks in case he meets Stepanida and is tempted. When Tolstoy had been married eight years, he was irresistibly attracted by still another handsome peasant girl, a servant in his house. Despite his sincere struggle to resist, he found himself one day making an assignation. On his way to keep it, his young son called from the window of his room to remind him of a Greek lesson he had promised, and this broke the spell of Tolstoy's desire—an incident that parallels one in *The Devil* where a servant interrupts Irtenev with a request from his wife when he is on his way to a rendezvous with Stepanida. And like Irtenev, Tolstoy tells a family tutor of his passion and begs his company on walks in order to save him from temptation should he meet the girl. This device, and the fact that Tolstoy soon arranged for his temptress to leave the estate, saved him.

Irtenev, however, despite marriage and fierce battles with his conscience, is unable to overcome his lustful desire for Stepanida, which in one sense may be considered a triumph of art over reality. The psychological analysis of Irtenev's obsession and of all the factors that lead him inevitably to his doom is an impressive and masterly performance.

Dissatisfied with the first ending, in which Irtenev kills himself, Tolstoy wrote a second in which the maddened lover, convinced after his hopeless struggle to tear Stepanida out of his life that she is a devil who has possessed him, murders her. Though opinions will naturally differ on their relative effectiveness, the second conclusion seems to satisfy better the demands of art as well as the ambivalence which has so profoundly wrenched the personality of Irtenev in its final stages of development.

As in *The Death of Ivan Ilych*, the emancipated realism of *The Kreutzer Sonata* shocked readers and also held them spellbound. Never before in Russian literature had sex, marriage, and the physical foundations of it been discussed so frankly. The initial idea for this short novel came from Tolstoy's friend, the actor V. N. Andreev-Burlak, who gave him an account of meeting a stranger on a train who told him the whole story of his wife's unfaithfulness. Tolstoy began his tale of "sexual love," as he called it, in 1887. The next year, a performance in his home by talented musicians of Beethoven's Kreutzer Sonata before a gathering that included Andreev-Burlak and the famous painter Repin suggested a new direction for the story that Tolstoy was working on. Music, it has been pointed out, often powerfully affected him, as it did on this occasion, and he promptly offered to write a story based on the sonata if the actor would agree to read it publicly in the presence of a canvas of Repin inspired by the music. Tolstoy alone fulfilled the agreement. In the course of writing *The Kreutzer Sonata*, however, it took on a deep personal significance for him. "The contents of what I wrote," he told a friend, "were as new to me as to those who read them. In this connection an ideal remote from my activity was revealed to me so that I at first became horrified and did not believe it, but then I grew convinced, repented, and rejoiced in what was to me and others a happy impulse."

The new ideal that had appealed to Tolstoy, for the expression of which his distraught hero Pozdnyshev in *The Kreutzer Sonata* became the mouthpiece, was the necessity of absolute chastity not only for unmarried, but even for married people. Though Tolstoy had previously advocated marriage as the only normal and moral outlet for sexual satisfaction, by 1888 his new faith, perhaps supported by his own mounting marital difficulties, caused him to repudiate his former beliefs in this respect. He declared to a disciple: "Man survives earthquakes, epidemics, terrible illnesses, and every kind of spiritual suffering, but always the most poignant tragedy was, is, and ever will be the tragedy of the bedroom." Scattered through *The Kreutzer Sonata* are various autobiographical echoes, such as Pozdnyshev's account of his loss of innocence when a mere boy, his ideas on premarital sexual relations and his youthful indulgence in them; turning over his diary, containing a record of his liaisons with women, to his bride-to-be; her disgust with the intimacies of the honeymoon; and later quarrels that developed between husband and wife over sex and the rearing of their children.

Though Tolstoy's original story of "sexual love" acquired some of the characteristics of a treatise on celibacy and chastity, his extraordinary artistic sense prevented it from turning into a mere didactic tract. Despite the half-mad behavior of Pozdnyshev nothing could be more realistically and psychologically compelling than the narrative of his moral and spiritual struggle against former personal convictions and the conventional taboos of society. The detailed account of the moves and countermoves and of all the reasons for them which step by step drive him on to kill his wife, and the description of the murder itself, are positively gripping. The story is an amazing example of Tolstoy's ability to elucidate a moral ideal of his own through the medium of artistic narrative.

What some critics, who identify Tolstoy's views with those

of his hero, fail to grasp is that Pozdnyshev's absolutist position on chastity, which if realized would end the human race, never remained more than an ideal for Tolstoy, a counsel of unattainable perfection in what he knew was an imperfect world. Constant striving for perfection was the only goal he had in mind. Nor did he entertain the illusion, as some imagined, that he of all people could achieve this ideal of chastity. Though cynical reviewers of *The Kreutzer Sonata* suggested that the author was getting old and that the grapes had turned sour, years later, when Tolstoy was nearly seventy, he told his translator, Aylmer Maude: "I was myself a husband last night, but that is no reason for abandoning the struggle. God may grant me not to be so again."

At first, *The Kreutzer Sonata* was denied publication in Russia, but manuscript copies and a lithograph version were circulated widely and commanded a high price as contraband literature. Its appearance in print did not take place until 1891, and then only through the efforts of Tolstoy's wife, who made a personal plea to Emperor Alexander III to be allowed to include it in the thirteenth volume of her husband's works which she was editing.

The Kreutzer Sonata caused more immediate public furor than any of Tolstoy's published works. A follower told him that friends on meeting, instead of saying "How do you do?" generally asked: "Have you read *The Kreutzer Sonata?*" The work has hotly debated everywhere and Tolstoy was deluged with letters, most of them disapproving. Some regarded it as an autobiographical account, as though Tolstoy had murdered his wife. Many accused him of preaching immorality and debauching the minds of the young. Priests gave sermons denouncing Tolstoy; a high government official urged the emperor to punish him; and the work was banned in the mails by the United States postal authorities.

In general, *The Kreutzer Sonata* fared badly at the hands of contemporary critics, largely because of its extreme views. However, the opinion of future critics was correctly antici- pated at the time by Chekhov, a most perceptive and objective judge in literary matters. Though Chekhov, a practicing physi- cian as well as a famous writer, took Tolstoy to task for his ignorance about doctors and scientists and for his erroneous statements in the work on syphilis, foundling hospitals, and women's aversion to sex, he declared of *The Kreutzer Sonata* that of all that was being written in Russia and abroad, "it is hardly possible to find anything of equal importance in con- ception and beauty of execution. Apart from its artistic merits which are in places amazing, we should be grateful for the story alone, for it stimulates thought extremely."

3

Walk in the Light While There Is Light (finished 1890; published 1893) and *Father Sergius* (finished 1898; published posthumously 1911) are short novels that bear a direct relation to the short moral and religious stories and legends that Tol- stoy wrote not long after his spiritual conversion. That is, they are much longer and more complex efforts to employ fiction to teach and illustrate the dogmas of Tolstoy's new faith. The purpose of the first is stated in its separate Introduction, enti- tled "A Talk Among Leisured People," in which a group of Tolstoy's own social class discuss the futility of their existence. Some insist that they abandon their property, labor as the common people do, and try to lead godly lives; others oppose this remedy as utterly impractical. The intention of the Intro- duction is not unlike the illustrative biblical quotations with which Tolstoy often began the short moral tales already men- tioned and discussed. The Introduction in this case, however, conjures up an imaginary scene, with some basis in fact, in which Tolstoy vainly pleads with his wife and family to give up their estate and genteel manner of life, live like peasants by the sweat of their brows, and by service and love for others come closer to God. The story that follows relentlessly exemplifies this teaching.

Walk in the Light While There Is Light is a tale of early Christian times during the reign of the Roman Emperor Trajan. It takes years and many bitter experiences before the rich man's son Julius comes to accept the Christian way of life advocated by his childhood friend Pamphilius. Both seek happiness, Julius in a conventional upper class pagan existence of careerism, dissipation, and indulgence in sex, Pamphilius by living simply, according to the teachings of Christ, in a small, industrious, but persecuted Christian community, believing that the welfare of all men lies in union with one another, a union attained not by violence, but by love. Though Tolstoy is obviously determined to offer an exposition of his own philosophy of life in the extensive discussions that take place between Julius and Pamphilius, he nevertheless argues both sides of the issue rather objectively and with unusual dialectical skill. As a matter of fact, the clear statement of Julius' position, fortified by arguments of the astute physician in the story on the attractions and superiority of the pagan way of life, quite unintentionally suggests some of the reasons why Tolstoy could never take the final step—as he earnestly wished to do—of leaving his home and family and going off somewhere to live like Pamphilius. Nevertheless, *Walk in the Light While There Is Light* is credited with influencing some Tolstoyan disciples to set up communes in which they would live according to the principles and practices of the Christian community described in the story, a development for which Tolstoy had no sympathy.

Later, in fact, Tolstoy frankly admitted that in this work he had subordinated artistic veracity to a form of tendentious teaching. "I never hear it mentioned," he told Aylmer Maude, "without feeling ashamed of myself. It is thoroughly inartistic. . . . In the story the Christians are all good and the pagans all bad, whereas in real life we know that they would have shaded off into one another as in the case of our own sectarians and Orthodox peasants." He is right. Such self-criticism is not infrequent in Tolstoy and is a hallmark of his greatness as a literary artist. For all his condemnation of the story, it has a number of fine passages and scenes that make it worth reading.

Though at the end of *Father Sergius* Tolstoy seems bent on pointing a moral implicit in his own faith, in general he avoids direct preaching in this short novel. The result is an absorbing study of spiritual pride which in a curious way is involved with carnal desire. Even if Tolstoy had wished to publish the work in his lifetime, its hard-hitting attacks on the shams and mercenary practices of the Church and the cynical behavior of the crown would probably have made it impossible.

The characterization of the complex Father Sergius is wholly convincing, both in the behavior pattern of his life and in the psychological justification of his actions and feelings. The dominant drives of pride and self-esteem in his nature help to explain why this brilliant young officer, well on the way to a major success in the service, suddenly decided to become a monk when he learns that the beautiful woman to whom he is engaged had been the mistress of the emperor. Because of his pride he had desired to look down on all those who considered themselves his superiors, and now at this devasting moment of failure in his career he thought that as a monk he could show contempt for everything that had formerly seemed important to him. Added to this he possessed a sincere religious feeling which, he felt, could also be a means of achieving the success he had forsaken in military service.

Though Father Sergius enjoys periods of religious exaltation in the early stages of his career in the Church, he fails to attain a state of mind and spirit free from the demands of vanity and the flesh. In despair he appeals for advice to a wise abbot under

whom he first served. This good man points out that he humili-
ates himself not for the sake of God, but for his pride, and he
recommends that Father Sergius go to a Tambov monastery
and there try to humble his pride by living as a hermit in a
cave.

What appears to be a turning point in his struggle with
doubts and desires of the flesh occurs when an attractive loose
woman, seeking excitement and pleasures, comes to his cave
and tries to seduce him. Tolstoy describes the scene with all
the power of his former realism. Overwhelmed by passion and
lust, Father Sergius, in a last desperate effort to mortify the
flesh, chops off his finger. Shaken by her gruesome experience,
the woman leaves and later enters a nunnery.

After this incident, sick people, attracted by the hermit's
religious strength of will, come to Father Sergius with pleas
that he heal them. In his pride he attempts to do this and soon
believes in his healing powers and enjoys his growing fame as a
holy hermit. Though he has moments when he realizes that he
does these things more for men than for God, he submits to the
desire of the monastery officials, who lucratively exploit his
reputation, that he make a kind of business out of performing
miraculous cures. But after succumbing to the blandishments
of a feeble-minded girl who is brought to his cell for treatment, Father Sergius, horrified by his sin, flees the monastery
dressed as a peasant.

Only at this point in his hero's tribulations does Tolstoy
appear to interfere. For the mystical experience Father Sergius
now undergoes, unlike those in *The Death of Ivan Ilych* and
Master and Man, seems more contrived than the outcome of a
natural welling up of spiritual forces under the compulsion of
some extraordinary human happening. An angel appears to him
in a dream and directs him to seek out a woman, a relation of
his whom he remembers as kind and selfless, always doing for
others despite the intolerable hard lot in life that fate has

accorded her. In his brief stay he learns from her self-sacrificing existence that she lives for God although she imagines that she lives for men, whereas he had been living for men on the pretext of living for God. Father Sergius leaves her to become a humble religious pilgrim. He has at last eradicated his pride. By attaching less importance to the opinions of the world of men, he feels more the presence of God within him.

4

Tolstoy found little leisure for fiction during the last few years of his life when much of his time was taken up by a multiplicity of cares connected with his new faith and by a steady stream of visitors from all over the world. In the light of such distractions from his art, it is interesting to come across an entry in his diary for July 17, 1896, which charmingly describes a walk he had just taken in the fields where he had observed a thistle broken by the plow but still alive, the flower in the center a vivid red. And he adds: "It reminded me of Hadji Murad. I want to write. Life asserts itself to the very end, and here in the midst of this whole field it has somehow asserted itself."

This passage contains the substance of the more elaborate and beautifully poetic beginning of his short novel *Hadji Murad* (finished 1904; published posthumously 1911), which in turn had been inspired by his seeing in the field the broken thistle with the live flower. A little more than a month later he drafted a sketch of the story, but he did not finish writing it until 1904 when he was seventy-six. It is one of his finest masterpieces.

In *Hadji Murad* Tolstoy, as an old man, returns to the memories of his youth in the Caucasus. Once in Tiflis in 1851, where he had gone to take an examination for a commision in the army, he met this half-wild Caucasian chieftain and wrote his brother Sergei of Hadji's surrender to the Russians: "He was the leading daredevil and 'brave' of all Circassia, but has been led to commit a mean action." In breaking with Shamil, who as head of all the hill tribes in the region had declared a Mohammedan holy war against the colonizing Russians, Hadji offered to lead his own followers against the enemy in return for Russian aid in buying the freedom of his family held as hostages by Shamil.

In preparing himself to write this story, Tolstoy refreshed his memory by reading everything he could get his hands on concerning the Caucasus, its people, and their struggle against the Russians. At moments he felt that he was wasting his time on "a mere work of art," but once, when parts of it were being read to guests at Yasnaya Polyana, he kept popping in and out of the room to listen, while urging them to cease bothering with such rubbish. "If that is so," one of the listeners demanded, "why did you write it?" And Tolstoy replied: "But it is not yet finished. You came into my kitchen and no wonder it stinks with the smell of cooking." Far from being "rubbish," *Hadji Murad* is perhaps his most perfect example of that "good universal art" which Tolstoy, in *What Is Art?*, had acclaimed as the highest form of fiction next to "good universal religious" literature.

Apart from remembered scenery and certain Russian soldier types, there is little else that Tolstoy draws upon from his youthful tales of army life in the Caucasus. In those early stories characters often see events through Tolstoy's eyes; in *Hadji Murad* his approach, for the most part, is quite objective, and the narrative structure is entirely different—a series of apparently separate scenes, but intricately connected, and narrated with studied simplicity and a minimum of literary adornment.

Hadji Murad is vividly portrayed, a brave person of great presence and dignity but at the same time shrewd and treacherous, a product of the virtues and faults of his savage environment. Hadji's confrontations with Tiflis high society are described with humor and irony. As a natural man he has nothing but contempt for the civilized artificiality of these aristocrats and government and military officials. And in the scene where Hadji's terms are presented to Emperor Nicholas I, Tolstoy amusingly satirizes the ruler, his bureaucrats, and court life in general. On the other hand, he invokes a poignant pathos in telling of the death in battle of a simple peasant soldier, whose old, hard-working mother, when she hears the news, weeps "for as long as she could spare the time," whereas his young wife, already pregnant by a shopman, remains indifferent to her husband's demise. The final tragic scene of the story, in which Hadji and several of his retainers, having escaped from the Russians, fight to the death scores of pursuers who surround them, is narrated with all the stark simplicity and precise detail of a great artist.

Entirely different in content, and somewhat in narrative method, *The Forged Coupon* (finished 1905; published posthumously 1911), which Tolstoy may well have begun or at least planned much earlier, is the last short novel he wrote. The complexity of its construction is unique for him in this genre, yet he handles it with superb skill. The motif running through the whole story is the evil-begetting power of evil which he had made such brilliant use of earlier in his remarkable play, *The Power of Darkness*. In *The Forged Coupon*, however, this motif is employed with a very different emphasis and purpose. An initial evil deed motivates a whole succession of evils, but these in turn are related to a series of good actions which eventually help to bring about the salvation of all the sinners concerned. In not a few of the situations, salvation is effected through the medium of Tolstoyan moral precepts.

The plan of the story requires a large number of characters. Though their varied activities are neatly tied together in rapidly shifting scenes which resemble a building-block type of structure, there is necessarily little characterization in depth, a fault perhaps inevitable in a short novel that contains more than enough material for a full-length novel. Tolstoy seems determined to expose all the crassness, meanness, and criminal tendencies of representatives of several layers of society—peasants, workers, shopkeepers, policemen, jailors, clergymen, magistrates, landowners, and government bureaucrats.

The central character and by far the most fully delineated is the peasant Stepan, whose murders are described with a macabre realism almost Dostoevskian in its intensity. This impression is especially marked in the account of his slaying Maria Semenova who lives by the Golden Rule and dies with pity for her murderer. Thereafter, her image haunts Stepan, and under its spell he goes through a mystical experience that compels him to surrender to the police and confess his crimes. In prison he is deeply influenced by a man whose religious teachings have a distinct Tolstoyan content. The spiritually and morally rehabilitated Stepan then becomes involved in activities which directly or indirectly help to alter the lives of a number of evildoers in *The Forged Coupon*.

If the conversions of some of these sinners seem at times more artificial than natural, Tolstoy offers the compensation of presenting a fascinating and varied picture of the Russia in which they live. And it has all the authenticity and verisimilitude of the consummate realism of the world-famous novels that he wrote many years earlier. In short, his powers of observation lost none of their acuteness in old age, nor did he lose the artistic urge to exercise them in enduring fiction. At the age of seventy-seven, only a few years before his death and while he was still probably working away at *The Forged Coupon*, he contemplated embarking on a huge novel that would have amounted to nothing less than a continuation of *War and Peace*. And he regretfully jotted down in his diary: "*Ars longa, vita brevis.* Sometimes I am sorry. There is so much I wish to say."

X

DRAMATIC WRITINGS

I

Tolstoy's international fame as a novelist has perhaps served to obscure his accomplishments as a playwright. He wrote no less than eight plays and dramatic sketches. Although there is evidence of his desire to succeed in the theater, he was never what might be called a "natural dramatist." Yet so rich and varied were his talents that even in this somewhat alien genre he did not fail to leave behind him traces of indubitable genius, and in his masterpiece, *The Power of Darkness*, one of the most impressive plays of the nineteenth century.

As a student in Kazan University the young Tolstoy acted with relish and ability in amateur theatricals. And when only twenty-eight we learn from his diary that the debauched surroundings of his village suggested to him the theme of a play: "Free Love." It would involve, he jotted down, the perverted relations of a "proprietress with her footman, a brother with his sister, and a father's natural son with the father's wife, etc." Fortunately, or perhaps unfortunately, in terms of Tolstoy's future literary image, only the bare beginning of this amazing dramatic design has survived in his manuscripts.

Tolstoy's first completed play is the little-known *Contaminated Family*, in five acts, which he wrote in 1864, very likely as a kind of relief from his arduous labors at that time on *War and Peace*. Its contents suggest that he had once again decided to pay off his radically minded critics, only now in a humorous, ridiculing manner, for the play depicts a typically vulgar group of representatives of the progressive movement of the 1860's. Among the principal characters is a landowner's daughter, with short hair, abbreviated skirt, dark spectacles, and a cigarette continually drooping from her mouth. In the jargon of the type, so celebrated in literature then, she regards herself as an "emancipated woman," scorns provincial aristocratic females and the "social web of prejudices," and while living off the substance of her wealthy uncle, she scorns him also. In addition, an ignorant, conceited, radical student, who imagines himself the most advanced of intellectuals, is amusingly satirized.

A Contaminated Family is a farce rather than a comedy, somewhat crude in stagecraft, but abounding in vitality, humanity, and common sense. For despite his personal sympathies, Tolstoy portrays his characters, who are fairly well individualized, with commendable impartiality, whether they belong to the new radicals or the old order of society.

Like any young dramatist with a first play, Tolstoy was eager to see it acted. With the encouragement of a relative, he went to Moscow to try and arrange the matter. As an initial precaution, he invited his acquaintance, the well-known professional playwright A. N. Ostrovsky, to hear him read *A Contaminated Family*. The growling, bearlike Ostrovsky let Tolstoy off lightly with the terse remark that the play had too little action and ought to be reworked, but to their mutual friend N. A. Nekrasov he wrote the unflattering comment: "It was so hideous that I positively had to stop my ears at his reading."

Tolstoy went blithely ahead and submitted the play for production, but he was informed by the theater that it was too near the end of the season to attempt a new piece. Shortly after, in a statement in a letter to his sister, it appears that he began to have second thoughts about his play, for he wrote: "Among other things I've done a comedy that I wanted staged at Moscow, but I had no success before Shrovetide, and the comedy, it seems, is poor; it was all written to ridicule the emancipation of women and the so-called nihilists." Actually, *A Contaminated Family* was never published or performed in his lifetime.

Two years later Tolstoy returned to the theme of nihilism. In the summer of 1866, on the occasion of a large gathering of family and their guests at Yasnaya Polyana, he proposed to the company that they do a little play for entertainment instead of the usual charades. They at once importuned him to write something, and several days later he brought them the manuscript of a comedy in three acts, entitled *The Nihilist*. The plot concerns a conventional married couple who are visited by a group of young people, one of whom is an attractive student obsessed by the new nihilist ideas. The husband imagines that the student has designs on his wife, but in the end, after some fetching fun-making at the expense of the youthful nihilist, all is satisfactorily explained. The roles were acted by the young people present, and after several days of rehearsing under Tolstoy's direction, *The Nihilist* was staged in the large dining room at Yasnaya Polyana, to the huge enjoyment of an audience composed of numbers of the household and neighbors.

2

Tolstoy did not soon follow up these two early attempts at playwriting with similar efforts, perhaps because he recognized then his inadequacies in the form, but more likely because of his deep involvement in *War and Peace* and shortly thereafter in *Anna Karenina*. However, the genre continued to fascinate him, especially as a literary form in which he had not yet achieved eminent success. When he returned to it twenty years later, his approach to playwriting, as to all forms of artistic expression, had been altered by the religious experience he had undergone in the meantime.

In 1886 the request of a well-known actor to rework some of his moral tales into plays for a people's theater prompted Tolstoy to turn once again to dramatic writing. He quickly produced a comedy, *The First Distiller,* a dramatization of his short story, "The Imp and the Crust." The several imps have no difficulty in ensnaring many members of the rich and idle classes for their master, the Devil. But the imp who is assigned to the peasants has no success at all because their lot of hard work remains a safeguard against sin. Only by teaching them how to make and drink vodka does the imp finally triumph over the peasants. This playlet, of course, is a forthright piece of temperance propaganda which, however, does not lessen its amusement when either read or acted. The scene where the peasants are corrupted by their first taste of liquor and lose their better judgment under its influence is executed with buoyancy and just enough realistic detail to sustain it on a high level of credibility.

During the same year (1886), another request, this time by the people's theater itself, led Tolstoy to write his grimly realistic tragedy, *The Power of Darkness.* It is based directly on the account of a crime he had heard several years before: a peasant confessed to the guests assembled at the marriage of his stepdaughter that he had murdered a child she had borne him and afterwards attempted to kill his own six-year-old daughter. Upon the foundation of this sordid crime Tolstoy built a moving drama that involved the darker aspects of peasant life. A good part of the play he wrote while he lay ill in bed with an infected leg. At times he would drop his pencil, throw his head back on the pillow, and his face took on an expression of the mingled pain of bodily and spiritual suffering that he experienced in creating horrific scenes dealing with adultery, murder, and infanticide. Once he admitted that he could never read without tears the scene in the cellar where Nikita crushed his child with a board so that its "bones crunched." The horror of it all, however, is strangely neutralized by the compulsion to atone for sin and by the moral message of the terrible evil-begetting power of evil, which is suggested in the play's subtitle: "If a Claw Is Caught, the Bird Is Lost."

The first act sets the main lines of the action, with no fumbling and with remarkable economy of effort, in the course of which are introduced all the principal characters in vivid, natural dialogue: the sickly husband Peter; his coarse-tongued, adulterous wife Anisya, who poisons him and marries her lover, the handsome, swaggering, village wencher Nikita; Anisya's slattern stepdaughter Akulina, whose illegitimate child by Nikita he and Anisya murder; Nikita's parents, the old God-fearing Akim, and Matryona, that triumph of wickedness, one of Tolstoy's great dramatic creations. Though he patently has no illusions about these peasants, we are convinced by the end of the first act that he feels deeply about them and, in terms of his new canons of art, he infects his readers with this feeling. As the play moves forward the feeling intensifies, and we share more and more the dramatist's concern for these men and women despite their tragic human weaknesses.

To compel belief in the action and characters of *The Power of Darkness*, Tolstoy employs some of the realistic subtleties of his earlier fiction, which he later condemned as superfluous in *What Is Art?* Though he has been criticized for reproducing a peasant dialect in the play, he had no alternative in the case of the men and women he portrayed. Thoroughly familiar with the peasant manner of speech, he artfully individualizes its peculiarities and intonations, in keeping with the personalities of the characters.

The power of suggestion achieved by contrast or juxtaposition of events or human attributes, so frequent in his novels, is brilliantly used to heighten tragic content in some of the great scenes in the play. As they try to go to sleep, old Mitrich, the rascally ex-soldier, tells Nan, Anisya's ten-year-old daughter, a story of fighting the Kurds and of capturing a little girl who becomes the pet of the regiment. At that moment we know—and Mitrich suspects—that Nikita's bastard child is being done away with only a few yards from them. And as we listen to the absorbing account about the little Kurdish girl, who used to hang around the neck of the old soldier after he had been flogged for drunkeness, we momentarily expect to hear the wails of the baby being murdered. There is also the scene of Matryona offering religious consolation to the dying Peter whom she had helped to poison, or that of her maternal tenderness to her distraught son Nikita after he has crushed his child to death, a deed which she had hounded him into doing. Then there is the striking episode of Nikita and Mitrich which George Bernard Shaw comments on: "I remember nothing in the whole range of drama that fascinated me more than the old soldier in your *Power of Darkness*. To me the scene where the two drunkards are wallowing in the straw, and the older rascal lifts the younger one above his cowardice and his selfishness, has an intensity of effect that no merely romantic scene could possibly attain."

The work soars to an impressive finale. With ineffable artistic appropriateness, Tolstoy places the truth of the play, its moral message of atonement for evil, in the mouth of old Akim, the least articulate of the characters. For after the conscience-striken Nikita's act of repentance in making public confession of his terrible crime, his father triumphantly declares to all: "God will forgive you, my own son! You have had no mercy on yourself. He will show mercy to you. God, God! It is He!"

The Power of Darkness has excellent acting qualities, and Tolstoy was anxious to have it staged as well as published, although he was aware that the official censor would hardly permit this. A friend and talented dramatic performer read the play with much success to Petersburg society gatherings at the beginning of 1887. He was then invited to give a reading of it to Alexander III and high court officials. The emperor seemed impressed, pronounced the play "a marvellous thing," and suggested that it be staged by the best actors and actresses of both Moscow and Petersburg theaters. Preparations went forward rapidly, until the plans were brought to the attention of K. P. Pobedonostsev, Procurator of the Holy Synod and archenemy of Tolstoy's new religious beliefs. He read the play and lost no time in writing to the emperor that *The Power of Darkness* filled him with horror and that it represented a "negation of ideals," a "debasing of moral feelings," and "an offense against taste." In his reply Alexander III judiciously recanted. He admitted that the play had made a strong impression on him, but that it had filled him with aversion and that it was his "opinion and conviction that it was impossible to stage the drama, because it was too realistic and frightful in its subject matter." With fickle royal favor withdrawn, the play could not be acted, although apparently through some oversight of the censor it was allowed to be published in 1887. A few weeks later the emperor sent a memorandum to the Ministry of the Interior: "One ought to put an end to this mischief of L. Tolstoy. He is a downright nihilist and atheist. It would not be bad now to forbid the sale of his drama, *The Power of Darkness*, for he has already succeeded in selling enough of his nastiness and in spreading it among the people."

Zola, in Paris, was less squeamish. In fact, he was enthusiastic over *The Power of Darkness* and arranged for its first performance in Paris in 1888. It was an overwhelming success and soon was running in three French theaters. Not until Alexander III's successor, Nicholas II, was the play certified for performance in Russia. At its opening in Petersburg (October 16, 1895) a capacity audience acclaimed Tolstoy, and aware of the victory he had won over the censors, they demanded that a congratulatory telegram be sent to the author. A little more than a month later the play was performed with equal success at the distinguished Maly Theater in Moscow. At its conclusion a crowd of students paraded to his house to pay tribute to him, and, filled with embarassment, he was unable for a few moments to say a word in reply.

3

It would be hard to imagine any greater contrast to the grimly tragic *Power of Darkness* than Tolstoy's next play, three years later, *The Fruits of Enlightenment* (1889). In the winter of that year the family remained behind at Yasnaya Polyana instead of moving to their Moscow home. The young people sought a play to perform to liven their evenings. One of Tolstoy's daughters recalled seeing the draft of a play among his papers. She purloined the manuscript and read it together with her sister and a young tutor in the family. It was just the thing—a merry comedy in four acts, in which high society and spiritualism were blisteringly satirized, while some wonderful peasant characters were introduced who provided a combination of farce and genuine distress over their lack of land. To the delight of the readers, they recognized among the characters members of the family, friends, and even some of their own peasants. Tolstoy, in contrast to his eagerness more than twenty years earlier to perform *The Nihilist* at Yasnaya Polyana, now remonstrated: staging a play, he said, was an amusement of rich and idle people. But the young folk stood their ground and soon the author was more deeply involved than his children. Though the search for God preoccupied Tolstoy during these later years, a spirit of fun, always characteristic of him and never far beneath the surface, willingly responded to the gaiety of those around him.

The trouble was that the play had thirty-one speaking characters. Soon telegrams were flying in all directions to summon friends and several absent members of the family. Parts were quickly cast and rehearsals went on daily. Tolstoy was nearly always present, directing and encouraging the actors, slapping his sides and wagging his head in peasant fashion, and laughing until the tears came when his humorous lines were effectively rendered. With animation he lectured the cast on dramatic art. During the rehearsals he attentively observed the performance of each actor and took notes on the dialogue. At night he collected all the roles, retired to his study, and altered the dialogue, sometimes adjusting it to the personalities of the players. These changes continued right up to the very performance of the work.

The Fruits of Enlightenment was first presented on December 30, 1889, before a sizeable audience of family, their guests, servants, and neighbors, and it achieved a triumphant success. It had been a long time since such jollity reigned in the great manor house of Yasnaya Polyana, which had been turned into a center of spiritual activity after Tolstoy's religious conversion.

The play received its first public performance at Tula, but was not produced in Moscow until 1891, and then, interestingly enough, by Stanislavsky, who was just beginning his noteworthy career as a director with his own company made up largely of amateur actors. According to Stanislavsky, "The performance was extraordinarily successful. The play ran till late spring, and helped us out of our financial difficulties." The next year Tolstoy saw it performed at the Maly Theater in Moscow, and it may be added that this play has held the boards in Russia ever since.

The Fruits of Enlightenment turns on a farcical situation in which a delegation of three peasants comes to the Moscow home of their wealthy master, Zvezdintsev, to persuade him to sell a large tract of village land which they desperately need for cultivation and grazing. Though he had formerly promised to do so, he now refuses because the peasants can afford only a small down payment on the total price. In the end, the maid, Tanya, who is engaged to the butler's assistant, Simon, whose father is one of the peasant delegation, tricks her master into signing the bill of sale at a spiritualism seance, then a popular fad among the gentry and one to which Zvezdintsev is passionately devoted.

Tolstoy contrives the situation in order to present a feverishly active gentry family living in the city with its swarm of servants, a representation not untypical of the time if we may judge from an abundance of concrete historical evidence as well as many other portrayals in nineteenth-century Russian belles-lettres. These utterly self-centered people are given entirely to pleasure and intellectual vulgarity. They and their social parasitism are effectively, and often humorously, contrasted to the servants and their hard-working way of life, and to the peasants with their concern for daily bread. Most of the characters are very much alive, especially the following: Zvezdintsev's cross-grained wife, Anna Pavlovna, who affects chronic illness and, convinced the peasant delegation is infected with diphtheria, drives them out of the house and has the room they occupy disinfected, and fires the butler because of his failure to cherish her lapdog Frisk, an animal she values above any of the servants; her son Vasily, who mocks the peasant delegation, lives solely for his membership in the Cycling Club, the Jockey Club, and the Society for Promoting the Breeding of Hounds; and the laughable Professor Krugosvetlov, whose erudition is employed more in the interests of self-deception in the practice of spiritualism than in the pursuit of truth.

The scenes belowstairs in the servant's quarters, where the peasants are made welcome, are expertly managed in action, dialogue, and characterizations. Their gossip reveals their own failings as much as it does the manner of life of the people they serve.

Tolstoy's moral bias and social criticism are plain enough. The peasants' urgent need for land—a lost cause that he never wearied fighting for—is highlighted, as well as the simple virtues of country life, which some of the servants long to return to, compared to the evil, wasteful existence of city dwellers. But these postures are not labored in the play. Though Tolstoy is bent upon satirizing the fecklessness and reprehensible behavior pattern of gentry and intellectuals, there is no meanness or bitterness in his many palpable hits. In fact, he brings out the human kindness of some of these upper class characters, as in the case of Betsy, Zvezdintsev's daughter, and his educated personal secretary, Fyodor Ivanich. Nor does he fail to poke fun at the follies and oddities of some of the servants and peasants.

The first two acts are full of life and reflect Tolstoy's obvious delight in creating characters that mean much to him; and he infects his readers with this delight. The final acts, however, tend to die on him, but not, as has been charged, because he betrays the characters in the end by his moralist's purpose. Rather, he excessively prolongs the denouement with altogether too much fussy business and detail when what was clearly called for was directness and simplicity in handling the conclusion.

4

Eleven years passed before Tolstoy attempted another play, *The Live Corpse* (1900). Several years previously, his friend N. V. Davydov, head of the Moscow District Court, had related to him the details of a curious case which inspired him to write *The Live Corpse:* A married couple in the city had separated, for the husband was a weak individual, addicted to drink, and the wife was in love with another man. In order to enable his wife to marry her lover, and apparently with her connivance, the husband simulated suicide by leaving his clothes and identification papers on the bank of the Moscow River. He then disappeared, and the wife married. But later, through an indiscretion of the vanished husband, the whole story came out and the couple were arrested and sentenced to a term of deportation.

Tolstoy was apparently dissatisfied with *The Live Corpse* and never subjected it to a final revision. When the theater director V. I. Nemirovich-Danchenko eagerly requested permission to produce it, Tolstoy refused. Aylmer Maude relates that Tolstoy told him that he did not wish the play to be performed while he lived, lest he should be drawn into expending time on revising it to the detriment of other tasks he considered more important. Another reason offered was that an account of *The Live Corpse* got into the press and was read by the first husband, N. S. Gimer, who appealed to Tolstoy not to publish the play since he feared to be compromised by it. Even the wife, through her son, is reported to have made a similar request, and Tolstoy willingly agreed, saying that "a human life is more precious than any piece of writing." It is known for certain that Gimer did visit Tolstoy, who aided him in obtaining work and exacted a promise from him never to touch liquor, which he kept. *The Live Corpse* was first published among Tolstoy's posthumous works in 1911 and was given its initial performance that year by Stanislavsky's Moscow Art Theater.

On the basis of the Moscow court case, Tolstoy erects a powerful psychological drama that seems to have only a tenuous connection with Davydov's account. Here he is in his literary element, dealing with upper-class men and women who might have appeared in *Anna Karenina*. Indeed, under different circumstances he might have turned this real-life situation into a full-length realistic novel as he did with another court case in *Resurrection*. With so expansive a theme, he struggles with the confining limitations of dramatic form, violating the conventions of the contemporary theater in piling up six acts, twelve scenes, and more than thirty speaking characters. Yet he meets the challenge with remarkable artistry, avoiding all non-essentials in projecting the actions and personalities of his men and women with the utmost frugality of means. The direct simplicity of his dialogue quickly individualizes the characters whose innermost unspoken thoughts are at times deftly suggested by precise stage directions, such as: "Karenin silently takes leave. . . . Lisa sighs and is silent."

Critical opinion on the merits of *The Live Corpse*, both in Russia and the West, varies considerably. In rereading the play for purposes of this appraisal, I found myself dissatisfied with a somewhat adverse judgment on it that I printed more than twenty years ago. The fact that Tolstoy wrote the play when he was over seventy has irresistibly attracted some critics to see in it reflections of his passionately held moral views at that time which, they claim, introduces a damaging subjective element into the work. Correctly read, however, the play yields little or no evidence of such false notes. It has been argued, for example, that Tolstoy wrote the play to demonstrate the harm that law—"government's organized instrument of coercion"—may do when it thrusts itself into the delicate relations of men and women. In a sense such a contention would place Tolstoy in a position of approving bigamy, however unintentional the crime is in the play. It is also maintained that he sacrifices the validity of his chief characters to his own personal moral position, although what that moral position is goes unstated by these critics unless it be the misfortunes that come from excessive addiction to liquor.

The truth of the matter is that the core of the play is an intensely human problem implicit in the nature of the given circumstances, and it is resolved with as much acute psychological insight as the central problem of *Anna Karenina*, to which it bears a certain resemblance. The breakup of the marriage of Fedya and Lisa is not really caused by his persistent drinking, but by the gnawing conviction that his wife, against her own intentions, has never ceased to love her childhood sweetheart, Karenin. "The very best love is unconscious love," Fedya tells Prince Abrezkov. "I believe she always did love him; but as an honest woman she did not confess it even to herself. But . . . a shadow of some kind always lay across our family life." And later Fedya declares to his drinking companion, Petushkov, that there was no yeast in their marriage, "there was never anything about her that made her creep into my soul. . . ." It is this pattern of frustration and not any innate moral weakness in his character that drives Fedya to drink and to leaving Lisa. Principles and integrity make it impossible for him to stoop to the lying and bribery necessary to obtain a divorce. At the suggestion of his gypsy friend, he goes through with the make-believe suicide in order to release his wife to marry Karenin, but only because he cannot take the terrible step of shooting himself. However, he unhesitatingly takes that step, after his simulated suicide is discovered, in the conviction that he must not stand in the way of the continued marital bliss of Lisa and Karenin.

No, *The Live Corpse* is quite free of Tolstoyan dogmatic moralizing, and Fedya is one of the most attractive and convincing characters in any of his plays. Moreover, one detects a quality of mellowness and deep sympathy for the erring ways of humanity in *The Live Corpse*, qualities which were rare enough in the creative works of Tolstoy's old age. The play is an altogether successful dramatic embodiment of a strange but real situation in life, and it is written with all the objective artistic skill of Tolstoy's literary genius.

5

In the few remaining years of his life Tolstoy attempted two more plays, of which the first, *The Light Shines in the Darkness*, is by far the most important. He appears to have begun it in the 1880's, put it aside for a long time, and then returned to it in 1900. By the end of 1902 he had finished four acts and left behind him detailed notes outlining the concluding fifth act.

Tolstoy obviously regarded *The Light Shines in the Darkness* as a significant work, for he wrote a friend: "It will contain my own experiences, my struggle, my faith, my sufferings—all that is close to my heart." In truth, the play reveals his later personal life more fully and more deliberately than any other creative effort of his, and, quite appropriately, as a consistently autobiographical work, he never wrote the last act.

The correspondences between the course of family life at Yasnaya Polyana after Tolstoy's spiritual change and that of the characters in the play are very close, but for artistic reasons he wisely allowed himself a considerable measure of creative inventiveness in this depiction. Yet his plain determination is to dramatize the essential domestic tragedy in his household during this period—to show how his wife, family, relations, friends, and social surroundings prevented him, intentionally or unintentionally, from living according to his convictions.

Within the limited scope of a play one obtains a rather vivid impression of what must have been the daily life of the Tolstoy family at Yasnaya Polyana and in their Moscow home. But the action is necessarily concentrated on the painful and often poignant efforts of Saryntsov (Tolstoy) to persuade his family of a deeply felt need to abandon his rather luxurious way of life and live according to his new morality and faith. Saryntsov hopes that his wife and children will join him in this endeavor, but only if their consciences move them to do so. The contentious dialogue that ensues among the many characters is weighted with defense of, or opposition to, typical Tolstoyan views on non-violence, the brotherhood of man, the practice of the golden rule, the virtues of providing for one's needs by labor, the chicanery of the church, and the evils of property, army conscription, and government coercion. Although Saryntsov argues that the search for truth is the one indubitable means of achieving the union of men, he understands clearly why people are not interested in the search and constantly misrepresent the truth. With unusual fairness Tolstoy strives to put in the mouths of various opponents of his hero telling arguments against his own position.

The real tension of the drama, however, is centered in the struggle of wills of Saryntsov and his wife. Saryntsov, tormented (as was Tolstoy) by the poverty and unprofitable toil of his landless peasants and the arrest of one of them for stealing timber he desperately needed, pleads with his wife to divide the estate, from which the family derives most of its income, among the peasants and to work to support themselves. Although she confesses to a friend: "What makes it so terrible is that is seems to me he is right," she understandably objects to her husband's proposal. How can she agree to beggar her numerous children, she asks, and she wonders why his particular form of Christianity requires that she ruin her whole family. Saryntsov is forced to compromise by deeding all his property over to his wife in a dubious effort to free himself of the guilt of possession. Indeed, compromises with his beliefs at every turn, out of a sense of duty to his family, are the main causes of Saryntsov's spiritual anguish.

On the whole, Saryntsov turns out to be a kind of Pippa in reverse; he passes through his own world of affairs and everything he touches he blights. He estranges his wife and children; a young priest he converts to his cause soon returns to the Church; Boris, another convert, engaged to Saryntsov's favorite daughter, refuses to serve his term in the army and perishes under punishment; and then the daughter marries a socialite whom her father detests. Moreover, in the notes for the unwritten last act, Saryntsov meets a rather futile end, for the outraged mother of Boris shoots him down. But before he dies, the notes indicate, he learns that the young priest has joined a religious sect sharing some of his mentor's views, and Saryntsov rejoices that the fraud of the Church has been exposed and that the priest has finally understood the meaning of his life.

One of the main troubles with the play is that Saryntsov never recommends himself to us as entirely real. It is as though Tolstoy, self-conscious about the autobiographical nature of the characterization, feared to evince any prejudices in the delineation. Saryntsov is rather cold, unsympathetic, and fanatical, in no way resembling the towering, life-loving, many sided genius of Yasnaya Polyana, who in real life never allowed the exacting logic of an ideal to reduce him to fanaticism. Looked at from another point of view, the portrayal of Saryntsov calls for a tribute to Tolstoy, for only a morally great man would employ the sincerity of art to depict himself so unmercifully. That is, if he could not sympathetically dramatize his spiritual struggle, he did reveal with devastating realism its harmful effects on all those he loved.

The Light Shines in the Darkness may well convince many of the futility of Tolstoy's nostrums when they are put into practice to solve the evils of the world. However that may be, this was clearly not his intention, as the notes for the last act suggest. His intention was to demonstrate that whatever may be society's opposition to his search for truth, the search was good and necessary, and the results, if sincerely acted upon, would be beneficial to mankind. The implication of the title of the play is that darkness, which does not comprehend the light, will one day vanish, and then all will see the light. George Bernard Shaw, who regarded the play as something of a masterpiece, put it in another way: "Nevertheless, Tolstoy does not really give the verdict against himself. He only shows that he was quite aware of the disastrousness of his negative anarchistic doctrine, and was prepared to face that disastrousness sooner than accept and support robbery and violence merely because the robbers and militarists had acquired political power enough to legalize them. It must be assumed that if everyone refused compliance, the necessities of the case would compel social reconstruction on honest and peaceful lines . . . he is a Social Solvent, revealing to us, as a master of tragic-comic drama, the misery and absurdity of the idle proud life for which we sacrifice our own honor and the happiness of our neighbors."

The final dramatic effort of Tolstoy, *The Cause of It All*, is a brutally realistic little vignette of peasant life in two short acts, which he wrote in 1910, not long before his death, for an amateur performance in the home of a disciple. It falls in the category of the moral tales that he began shortly after his religious conversion, and is designed to show the evils of drink and how human kindness can bring out the best in the lowliest of God's creatures. But the moral element is lost sight of in the swiftly developing action in the peasant's hut, where the tipsy husband and his friend arrive from the market and find a tramp wished on the household for the night by the village elder. In the drunken scene that follows, the tramp, a proletarian revolutionary type given to "expropriating" money for the good of the cause, saves the nagging wife from a beating by her husband. In the morning the tramp is caught with the package of tea the husband had bought at the market, and now it is the wife who performs the kindness, pleading that he not be turned over to the police. Her husband, not to be outdone by his wife, not only frees the tramp, but insists that he take the tea with him. Finally, the tramp touched to tears by their generosity, rails against himself as a scoundrel, leaves the package of tea on the table, and quietly goes his way. "How he cried, poor soul," remarks a neighbor after the tramp's departure, and the old peasant grandmother softly adds the moral: "He too is a man." Slight as it is, *The Cause of It All*, in its realistic details and wonderfully natural dialogue, shows that Tolstoy, even at the age of eighty-two, had lost none of his artistic touch.

6

Six of Tolstoy's eight plays, including his artistically most important, were all written after he had developed his new religious and moral outlook on life. Hence it is rather surprising to find him declaring in *Shakespeare and the Drama* (1906): "I myself have incidentally written for the theater. I recognize them [his plays], just like all the rest, to be lacking in that religious content which should form the basis of the future drama." One would assume from this that he regarded his plays as "incidental" in the total corpus of his artistic works, and that they lack a pronounced religious content, which the foregoing examination of them has been concerned to demonstrate, particularly in the two best ones—*The Power of Darkness* and *The Live Corpse*.

Fundamentally, Tolstoy's approach to playwriting was the realistic one of his fiction, and it is difficult to imagine what he might have accomplished if he had elected to devote major attention to the genre in his extraordinary earlier creative period, before the free expression of his artistic powers became somewhat fettered by moral and religious considerations. Despite significant achievements in his finest plays, he was not a born innovator in drama. In his later years he denounced Russian playwriting as "merely an empty and immoral amusement." Though this opinion had some point at that time, it is indicative of his inadequacies as a playwright and critic of the theater that he could not correctly evaluate the few efforts being made then to write and perform plays that had fresh, innovating approaches to the art.

Among these new approaches was Chekhov's, and though Tolstoy had the highest admiration for him as a writer of short stories, he seemed utterly incapable of appreciating his famous plays. Although he laughed uproariously upon seeing the early conventional one-act plays of Chekhov, such as *The Wedding* and *The Bear*, he damned *The Sea Gull*, which he read, and *Uncle Vanya*, which he saw acted. "Where is the drama?" he asked one of the actors after the performance of *Uncle Vanya*. "In what does it consist?" The action never moved from one place, he complained, and Uncle Vanya and Astrov, he declared, were simply good-for-nothing idlers who had escaped from real life into the country as a place of salvation.

What particularly troubled Tolstoy, as he indicated in an interview shortly after Chekhov's death, was Chekhov's attempt to use a play instead of a lyrical poem to evoke a poetic mood. This confusion in form, Tolstoy suggests, results in the spectator being asked to pity Uncle Vanya and Astrov without ever being informed by the dramatist whether or not they deserve pity. (Here speaks the everlastingly logical Tolstoy, who believed that art should never conceal but reveal, that the reader or spectator should never have to wonder or guess at the author's intention.) Nor could he see any purpose in *Uncle Vanya*, or, for that matter, in *The Sea Gull* and *The Three Sisters*, which he could not finish reading. With the conventional drama of direct action in mind, Tolstoy expected a play to deal with moral problems of society, and the characters involved in them to be portrayed in terms of their developing personalities through the actions and related dialogue. These expectations, which were shared by many of Tolstoy's contemporaries, were entirely foreign to what Chekhov was trying to do in his four famous plays of indirect action.

Chekhov was aware of Tolstoy's dislike of his plays, but his unfailing sense of humor and devotion to him would hardly have allowed him to be offended. He told a young writer of Tolstoy's frank opinions in this respect: "You know, he does not like my plays. He swears I'm not a dramatist. There is only one thing that comforts me. . . . He said to me: 'You know, I cannot abide Shakespeare, but your plays are even worse. Shakespeare, after all, grabs the reader by the scruff of the neck and leads him to a certain goal, not permitting him to wander off the road. But where are you going with your heroes? From the divan to the outhouse and back?'" At this point in his account, Chekhov laughed so hard that his pince-nez fell off his nose. "But really, Leo Nickolaevich was serious," Chekhov continued. "He was ill. I sat with him at his bedside. When I began to get ready to leave, he took my hand, looked me in the eye, and said: 'Anton Pavlovich, you are a fine man.' Then smiling, he let my hand go and added: 'But your plays are altogether vile.'"

X I

RESURRECTION

During the second half of 1899 the atmosphere of the Tolstoy household was tense over the mighty effort to complete *Resurrection* which was then appearing serially in a magazine. Racing against time in the face of pressing telegrams from the editor for next week's copy, the seventy-one-year old author, deserting his family, shut himself up in his study for days on end, taking his meals at odd hours, and refusing to see visitors. Always the exacting artist, he kept mangling successive sets of proof, repeatedly rewriting whole sections, and hurrying off last-minute changes for an installment just about to go to press. Fresh manuscript chapters in his almost illegible handwriting were cleanly copied by members of the family and their guests. Duplicate sets of corrected proof had to be prepared for translators for foreign publication. Urgent cablegrams and letters from abroad offered huge sums for first publishing rights. Finally, on December 18, Tolstoy noted in his diary: "Completed *Resurrection*. Not good, uncorrected, hurried, but it is done with and I'm no longer interested."

Tolstoy's sense of relief may be partly attributed to the fact that he had been working away intermittently on *Resurrection*, the last of his three great full-length novels, for more than ten years. The theme had been supplied by his good friend, the eminent jurist and writer A. F. Koni. He told Tolstoy the story of a man who had come to him for legal aid. As a youth this man had seduced a pretty orphan girl of sixteen who had been taken into the home of a relative of the young man when her parents died. Once her benefactress observed the girl's pregnant condition, she drove her away. Abandoned by her seducer, the girl, after hopeless attempts to earn an honest livelihood, became a prostitute. Detected in stealing money from one of her drunken "guests" in a brothel, the girl was arrested. On the jury that tried the case fate placed her seducer. His conscience awakened to the injustice of his behavior, he decided to marry the girl, who was sentenced to four months in prison. Koni concluded his story by relating that the couple did actually marry, but shortly after her sentence expired, the girl died from typhus.

The tale deeply moved Tolstoy, and its effect may well have been connected with an acute stirring of conscience. For shortly before his death he told his biographer of two seductions in his own life which he could somehow never forget. "The second," he said, "was the crime I committed with the servant Masha in my aunt's house. She was a virgin. I seduced her, and she was dismissed and perished." At first he urged Koni, a very talented person, to publish the account for *Intermediary*, the firm that Tolstoy established to market inexpensive moral booklets for the masses. Koni agreed to do this. When a year passed and he failed to fulfil his promise, Tolstoy asked to be allowed to make use of the story.

Tolstoy's efforts to cast this incident of real life into literary form were repeatedly interrupted by the manifold activities and extensive polemical writings growing out of his spiritual revelation. Only with some reluctance did he devote his few free hours to the creation of fiction, and it is possible that *Resurrection* might never have been finished if it had not been for a special set of circumstances. The government's long and cruel persecution of the Dukhobors, a peasant sect that practiced a form of Christian communism not far removed from Tolstoy's own preaching, and among other things rejected military service, had reached a crucial stage. For several years he and his followers had been aiding the Dukhobors. Now it was decided that the most practical remedy for their misfortunes was to have them emigrate. The Russian government was willing, and Canada agreed to accept them pretty much on their own terms. The problem was to obtain money to transport and settle in Canada some twelve thousand sectarians. Tolstoy helped to organize a campaign to raise funds. Although he had surrendered the copyrights of all his works written since his spiritual change and allowed anyone to publish them free, he now decided to sell a novel and devote the proceeds to the fund to aid the emigration of the Dukhobors. Going over his portfolio of unfinished manuscripts, he settled upon *Resurrection* as the one calculated to earn the most money, and he set to work with a will to complete this long novel.

Before the serial publication had got well under way in the magazine *Niva*, Tolstoy began to regard his compact with the publisher as one with the devil—he had sold his soul for an advance of twelve thousand roubles, even though the money went to the fund for the Dukhobors. This only instance of violating the repudiation of his copyright privileges to the extent of accepting money for the initial publication of a novel caused him endless trouble. *Niva* at first attempted to run the lengthy work in weekly installments. With his painstaking correction of proof and the constant introduction of new matter, Tolstoy found it extremely difficult to keep up this pace. Finally his health broke down and he virtually decided to end the novel with Part II, omitting the brilliant third part. Only the willingness of the editor to forego his demand for weekly installments persuaded Tolstoy to continue.

2

Tolstoy had calculated correctly. The first full-length novel in twenty years from the celebrated author of *War and Peace* and *Anna Karenina*, and also a man now universally known as a religious reformer and moral thinker, was an event of intense international interest. While *Resurrection* was appearing serially in Russia, simultaneous publication in translation was arranged in England, France, Germany, and the United States. Partly because of the previous public repudiation of his copyright privileges, much pirating went on which caused Tolstoy a great deal of embarrassment—he had sold first publication rights to various foreign firms in an effort to realize the maximum income on behalf of the Dukhobors. Pirated copies of the novel quickly appeared in Russia; twelve different translations came out in Germany alone in 1900; and fifteen editions, under authorized and unauthorized imprints, accumulated in France during 1899 and 1900. Extreme liberties were often taken in these foreign versions. When French readers of the serialized translation in *Echo de Paris* characteristically complained that the love scenes, which they relished, were too infrequent, the businesslike editor had no scruples about omitting the next regular installment and substituting for it one in which the hero and heroine were again occupied with each other. On the other hand, the editor of *Cosmopolitan*, which had bought first serial rights in the United States, did not hesitate to tone down or delete love passages which he thought might offend the sensibilities of this magazine's respectable middle-class readers. In the end, Tolstoy was happy to revert to his rule of not taking money for his writings, unwilling perhaps to realize that the rule itself had been the cause of all his trouble.

The Russian censor caused additional annoyance and not a little anguish to Tolstoy, who in some instances protested the deletions of this high executioner of words. The censor, however, could hardly be expected in those days to tolerate the author's sacrilegious barbs against the Russian Orthodox Church or his exposure of the way prisoners were treated in Siberia. In fact, very few of the many chapters of the novel escaped the censor's awful blue pencil, and it is estimated that be made four hundred and ninety-seven separate alterations or deletions in the text. Not until 1936 did the complete and unaltered text of *Resurrection* appear in Russian, in the huge Jubilee Edition of Tolstoy's works.

In the course of writing the novel, Tolstoy did considerable research, reading many books and articles—he read six books on prostitution alone—and he consulted experts on legal procedure, visited jails and talked with convicts. Once he got fairly into the work, it absorbed him completely, and he told his wife that since *War and Peace* he had never been so powerfully gripped by the creative urge. Koni's slender narrative served only as the initial inspiration for the erection of a huge, complex superstructure, and as in the case of Tolstoy's other two large novels, the story element grew to formidable length, with numerous ramifications. There were several quite different beginnings, and again and again he cast out themes and introduced entirely new ones. Even such a small detail as the description of the external appearance of the heroine exists in as many as twenty variants. There were six separate redactions of *Resurrection*, and before Tolstoy had finished his extensive revisions, he had piled up enough rejected material to fill a volume almost as large as the novel itself.

As in Tolstoy's previous full-length novels, there is a great

deal of autobiographical matter in *Resurrection*. In many respects the hero, Dmitri Nekhlyudov, resembles his creator, and
a number of the other characters are plainly modeled on people
Tolstoy knew. For example, Toporov is a thinly disguised and
unflattering portrait of the sinister and celebrated Procurator
of the Holy Synod, K. P. Pobedonostsev. Some of these autobiographical aspects are curiously stressed in an interesting
passage in the diary of Tolstoy's wife. While wearing her eyes
out over recopying his labyrinthine manuscript, she vented her
spleen against *Resurrection* largely because her husband had
refused first publishing rights for her edition of his works—it
may be remembered that he had previously allowed her the
right to publish for money anything he wrote before his spiritual revelation, that is, before 1881. "I torment myself," she
wrote, "over the fact that Leo Nikolaevich, a seventy-year-old
man, describes the scene of fornication between the serving girl
and the officer with the peculiar relish of a gastronome eating
something tasty. I know, because he himself told me about this
in detail, that in this scene he is describing his own intimate
relations with the serving girl of his sister. . . . I'm also tormented by the fact that I see in the hero, Nekhlyudov,
portrayed as progressing from his downfall to his moral resurrection, Leo Nikolaevich, who thinks this very thing about
himself."

Abroad, especially in England and the United States, *Resurrection* was enthusiastically received and enjoyed a larger sale
than any other work by Tolstoy up to that time. Though some
conservative foreign critics expressed indignation over what
seemed an excessively frank and un-Victorian treatment of sex,
as well as the novelist's contemptuous regard for the conventions of law and order and the sacredness of the church,
progressive critics showered praises on perhaps the only man in
Russia at that time who had the courage to expose in fiction the
evils that beset his country. In Russia the publication of *Resur-*

rection was an event transcending its artistic significance. Something of the widespread excitement aroused by the novel as it appeared serially is reflected in a letter to Tolstoy by his friend V. V. Stasov, a distinguished art critic: "How all of us here rejoiced when we learned that the chapters of *Resurrection* will not be 60 or 80 but 100 or more. Without exception all are saying on every side: 'Ah, there will be more, more will be added! May God grant that there will be more and more!'"

3

Resurrection naturally forces comparison with those supreme works, *War and Peace* and *Anna Karenina*, and it must be admitted that it falls below the lofty artistic achievements of these earlier novels. However, its best things, artistically speaking, belong to the narrative method of Tolstoy's earlier fiction rather than to the compressed, direct, and stylistically unadorned manner of the later period after *What Is Art?* was written. In *Resurrection* there is that same wealth of precise realistic detail which conveys the appearance of indubitable actuality to imagined situations, as well as roundness, completeness, and the vitality of life to his characters. In its enchanting setting, the account of the first pure love of Nekhlyudov and Katusha Maslova, certainly the finest section of the novel, is all compounded of that same wonderful elusive quality that transformed the girlish loves of Natasha in *War and Peace* into the incommunicable poetry of youthful dreams. Tolstoy never did anything more delightfully infectious in fiction than the scene of the Easter service in the village church, where the young hero and heroine, after the traditional Russian greeting "Christ is risen," exchange kisses with the carefree rapture of mingled religious exaltation and dawning affinity for each other.

There is much of the old master also in Tolstoy's handling of the trial scene, in the portrayal of high society in both Moscow and Petersburg, and in the remarkably realistic treatment of the brutal march of the convicts to Siberia. In this area, however, the satirical representations of society are much less objective, and more grim and didactically purposeful than anything in *War and Peace* and *Anna Karenina*. Herein, indeed, lies the major artistic fault of Tolstoy's last full-length novel.

While he was writing *War and Peace* Tolstoy, troubled by the thought that the radical critics would attack him for failing to expose the faults of the privileged classes and the dark misery of the peasantry in his work, wrote to a friend to defend his avoidance of social problems: "The aims of art are incommensurable (as they say in mathematics) with social aims. The aim of an artist is not to resolve a question irrefutably, but to compel one to love life in all its manifestations, and these are inexhaustible. If I were told that I could write a novel in which I could indisputably establish as true my point of view on all social questions, I would not dedicate two hours to such a work; but if I were told that what I wrote would be read twenty years from now by those who are children today, and that they would weep and laugh over it and fall in love with the life in it, then I would dedicate all my existence and all my powers to it."

Some thirty years later Tolstoy turned his back on this admirable credo of relative objectivity in art in writing *Resurrection*—an unashamedly purpose novel. To be sure, most great novels are in one sense or another purpose novels, but the purpose is sublimated in a depiction of life free of any special pleading that distorts the essential artistic unity of the whole. In *Resurrection* Tolstoy's purpose of condemning the violence of government, the injustice of man-made laws, the hypocrisy of the Church, and of pleading the biblical injunction to judge not that you be not judged, obtrudes in a rather scholastic manner throughout the novel.

In fact, *Resurrection* is in many respects an amazingly accurate portrayal of the spiritual biography of Tolstoy, and though this may detract from it as an artistic performance, it provides rich and authoritative material for all who wish to understand the tremendous moral and religious struggle of one of the foremost thinkers in the latter half of the nineteenth century. For the essence of much that Tolstoy thought and suffered during and after his spiritual travail is condensed in the pages of this novel.

Nekhlyudov's youthful idealism, forgotten in a subsequent period of debauchery in the army and in high society, which in turn is followed by a spiritual crisis, moral suffering, and an intense search for the meaning of life, is a pattern of development that Tolstoy himself experienced. Although there are certain autobiographical elements in the immediate cause of the crisis, the soul-searing confrontation of Nekhlyudov with the prostitute Katusha Maslova at her trial for robbery and murder, ten years after he seduced her as a pure young girl, is based on the stuff of Koni's real-life story. But the handling of the theme from this point on is done entirely in terms of the religious, moral, and social convictions that Tolstoy eventually arrived at after his own conversion.

Despite this rather doctrinaire approach, the resolution of the future relations between Nekhlyudov and Katusha is worked out with considerable psychological subtlety. The hero recognizes, as does Katusha after being unjustly convicted, that his initial determination to follow her to Siberia and marry her is simply an attempt at self-sacrifice to atone for having started her on her wayward path. Before this action can come from the heart, before it can be purged of every aspect of self-interest, sentimentality, and conscious do-goodism, he must undergo his own Golgotha on the way to achieving a new faith where practice of the golden rule is instinctive and not calculated. His example and patient ministrations also begin to work a moral change in Katusha, and this transformation is completed by her harsh prison experiences, in the course of which she learns from some of her fellow convicts, especially among the political prisoners, the true dignity of man. Katusha's original pure love for Nekhlyudov is restored. Here, in the struggle between the truth of the moralist and the truth of the artist in Tolstoy, the artist prevails. He makes no concession to the conventional happy ending of virtue rewarded, for Katusha ultimately refuses to marry Nekhlyudov. She senses that she will only be a hindrance to the work that he must do in the world in living according to his new faith, and she gives up this happiness by deciding to share in marriage the life of one of her fellow prisoners who loves her with an entirely platonic love. Sex, indeed, is the inevitable victim of the higher synthesis of the Tolstoyan life of the spirit.

In the many scenes, often brilliantly realized, in the courts, the prisons, in Nekhlyudov's dealings with his peasants, and in the homes of high society, rarely is the moralizing element unadorned by abundant trappings of real life. However, these scenes, through which Nekhlyudov sometimes moves like a somnambulist, often appear to be contrived indictments of various aspects of Russian society designed to explain and justify the hero's spiritual resurrection. For every abuse revealed and for every moral corrective administered, chapter and verse may be found in the various controversial books and articles that Tolstoy had already written on these subjects. The positions taken are argued with all his consummate skill, and irony and paradox are employed most effectively. Yet, in some of these passages, Tolstoy, either as the omniscient author or through the mouths of his characters, seems to be searching for absolutes in a world of incomplete knowledge and imperfect men. Occasionally there are lapses of tasts, as in the blasphemously satiric account of the Russian Orthodox Church service, and at least once he fails to grasp the historic significance and political thinking of a whole group of characters he introduces—the revolutionary intelligentsia.

Among the scores of secondary characters in *Resurrection,* hardly any lack that baffling artistic touch of definition and individualization which dazzled readers and critics alike in the great novels of Tolstoy's earlier period. However fleeting their roles may be, the judges and jurymen at the trial, the amazing women inmates of Katusha's cell, and the various political prisoners are brought to life with a few deft strokes of description and psychological observation. And still more memorably characterized are those creatures of high society and official Moscow and Petersburg life—the Korchagin family, especially the mother and her daughter Missy who vainly hopes to marry Nekhlyudov; the cynical advocate Fanarin who symbolizes the irrelevance of justice in the courts of law; the Vice-Governor Maslenikov whose official duties are regarded as mere appendages to social climbing; and the general's pretty wife Mariette whose delicate suggestions of a liaison with Nekhlyudov he regarded as a more reprehensible and much less honest approach than that of the streetwalker who had accosted him.

The story of *Resurrection,* however, is overwhelmingly the story of Nekhlyudov, who is imbued with his creator's instinct to discover the purpose of life. In the first part of the novel the hero emerges as a rather fascinating man of action who engages our sympathies in his developing personality. As a member of the gentry—Tolstoy's own class which he knew so well—Nekhlyudov has many of the appealing traits found in Prince Andrew in *War and Peace* and Vronsky in *Anna Karenina.* But unlike these characters, Nekhlyudov is soon confronted by a crisis that transforms him into an intellectual Tolstoyan, a development that seems false to his nature, and more dictated by the author than by life. In the remainder of the novel he is more acted upon than active in a series of situations patently designed to aid him in his search for the meaning of life. And he finds it in the end, very much as Tolstoy did, in the Sermon on the Mount. "A perfectly new life dawned that night for

Nekhlyudov," the novel concluded, "not because he had entered into new conditions of life, but because everything he did after that night had a new and quite different meaning for him. How this new period of his life will end, time alone will prove."

This hint at a sequel to the novel has some basis in fact, for shortly after he finished it, Tolstoy wrote in his diary: "I want terribly to write an artistic, not a dramatic, but an epic continuation of *Resurrection:* the peasant life of Nekhlyudov." Apparently in his new existence the hero was to play the part of a peasant, perhaps a successful Tolstoyan peasant, which would have been unique in either fiction or life. But Tolstoy never lived to complete this grand design.

According to Tolstoy's principal criterion of real art, namely, infectiousness, which he developed in his treatise *What Is Art?*, *Resurrection* holds up quite well. That is, the novel deals with feelings sincerely expressed by the author, and so artistically conveyed that they infect readers and cause them to share these feelings with him and with each other. And certainly more than any of his other novels, *Resurrection* fulfils Tolstoy's definition of the best art, for it evokes in us feelings of brotherly love and of the common purpose of the life of all humanity—a striving to achieve spiritual and moral perfection through service to others.

XII

TOLSTOY'S IMAGE
TODAY

I

In November, 1910, Leo Tolstoy lay dying in the stationmaster's house at Astapovo, a tiny railroad siding in the center of Russia. One of his children bent down to catch the almost inaudible last words of her aged father: "To seek, always to seek . . ." Then this articulate voice of the conscience of humanity, the symbol of mankind's endless struggle for moral improvement, ceased forever. The press of every country anxiously waited for information concerning the illness of the world's foremost literary figure. Finally, the flash came: "Tolstoy is dead!" A hush fell over hundreds of thousands of people who had been patiently standing before the news centers throughout the cities and towns of Russia. Young and old removed their hats. Many wept softly.

Tolstoy's voice as the conscience of humanity has become a still small one since 1910, although it resounded loudly once again among a group of distinguished thinkers, writers, and scholars, representing a dozen countries, who gathered in an international conference in November, 1960, to commemorate the fiftieth anniversary of the great man's death. The setting was an austere hall of the ancient Benedictine monastery on the lovely little island of San Giorgio Maggiore, set like a bright jewel in the sun-drenched shimmering green lagoon directly opposite the fabulous San Marco shoreline of Venice, that "strange dream upon the water." High upon the back wall of the conference room an enormous canvas of the school of Tintoretto, depicting the mystic marriage of the Virgin, looked down piously on some fifty participants who for days poured forth a torrent of words in four languages on the art and thought of a man whom the Church, in his own day, had denounced as an "anathematized atheist and anarchist revolutionist" and "an accursed and most disdained Russian Judas." With his intense dislike of all organized efforts to honor him, Tolstoy—if he had been alive—would no doubt have pleaded that this conference be abandoned, as he publicly pleaded on the occasion of the vast national plans to celebrate his eightieth birthday. He would appreciate it more, he declared at that time, if the government would throw him into prison instead of persecuting his followers, and into "a real good stinking prison—cold and hungry." Tolstoy always felt humiliated at being a kind of modern-day Christ without a cross to bear.

The universal deterrence of fear which contributes so profoundly to our anxieties over the state of the world today no doubt served to focus the thoughts of many of the conference participants on Tolstoy's conviction that the tendency to replace moral and spiritual progress by technical progress is one of the main calamities of modern life. Indeed, the presence of several eminent Soviet Tolstoyan scholars inevitably resulted in the introduction into the discussion of cold-war overtones. Tolstoy's works are proudly acclaimed by the Soviet Union as among the greatest in the country's artistic heritage from the past. And 1960 was designated as the "year of Tolstoy" in the Soviet Union. Celebrations throughout the country were held, involving many fresh editions of his works and of books about him, theatrical performances, music, cinema, exhibitions, several thousand lectures, learned conferences, the unveiling of monuments, and a huge concluding commemorative meeting in the Moscow Bolshoi Theater, which was attended by government leaders and distinguished writers, artists, and scientists.

There can be no question of the reverence of Soviet people for Tolstoy, but the official position of the Communist party is compounded of praise and that familiar moral shuffling in ideological matters that is at once naïve and offensive to all who pursue historical truth. If Soviet pundits praise him for subjecting the very foundations of his own society to devastating criticism, they condemn him for rejecting the historical necessity for real struggle.

It is safe to assume that Tolstoy, had he lived, would have discerned no essential difference between the authoritarian government of the tsars and that of the Kremlin. He fully realized that brutality, injustice, tyranny, and exploitation committed in the name of the "people" or religion or ideology were no better than brutality, injustice, tyranny, and exploitation perpetrated by feudal lords or capitalist exploiters. Economic ideals, he once said, could never be real ideals, and he saw that the mistake of the Marxists and of the whole materialist school was in believing economic causes to be at the root of all problems, whereas the life of humanity was really moved by the growth of consciousness and religion. And with surprising prescience he pointed out a further danger in communist revolution. The one sphere of human life which governmental power did not encroach upon—the domestic, economic sphere—"thanks to the efforts of socialists and communists, will be gradually encroached upon, so that labor and recreation, housing, dress, and food (if the hopes of the reformers are fulfilled) will all gradually be prescribed and allotted by the government."

Soviet critics today either ignore this negative position on the future of communism or else adopt Lenin's line on Tolstoy of differentiating between the virtues of the artist and the faults of the philosopher. Occasionally they also profess to see in the novels an implicit faith in the triumph of a world-wide brotherhood of men which they hope the reader will identify with the ultimate aims of communism. To be sure, there is a certain identity in the final aim of both—a classless and stateless society. As one contemporary revolutionist put it to Tolstoy in his Marxian phraseology: "You use the tactic of love and we use that of violence. . . ." But it was just this violence which creates violence, the evil-begetting power of evil, that Tolstoy could not tolerate as a substitute for his eternal law—the "tactic of love." He once coarsely explained to an eager antagonist, who insisted on the moral difference between the killing that a revolutionist does for the sake of the masses and that which a policeman does: "There is as much difference as between cat shit and dog shit. But I don't like the smell of either one or the other."

2

Western critics today also tend to make an unfavorable distinction between Tolstoy, the supreme literary artist of *War and Peace* and *Anna Karenina*, and the Tolstoy who, after his spiritual revelation in 1880, turned his back on art and became the cranky preacher of an uncompromising and impractical moral philosophy, a kind of latter-day prophet tiresomely warning the world that if his prescriptions for its social and moral ills were not heeded, the very existence of civilization would be threatened.

As we have seen, Tolstoy did not actually turn his back on

art after 1880. Many artistic works were still to come from his pen, including such memorable efforts as *The Death of Ivan Ilych, Resurrection, Hadji Murad,* his best plays, and the superb moral tales. It is nonsense to imagine that the great literary artist before 1880 suddenly transformed himself into a kind of intellectual crackpot once he began to seek an answer to that tremendous problem: What is the meaning of life? All the moral and spiritual searching and intellectual and artistic direction of his being after 1880 were plainly suggested in his youthful diaries, letters, and early artistic writings. After his spiritual revelation, however, these factors underwent, not a change, but a significant development. When Turgenev pleaded with him to return to the literary art that had first won him fame, he did not understand that for Tolstoy the measure of true greatness was not what we were but what we strove to be in the ceaseless struggle to achieve moral perfection. Nor did Turgenev comprehend that the same magnificent qualities that made Tolstoy's art immortal—his sincerity and love of truth—were the very qualities that drove him on in his religious and social mission. No, the search had to continue.

To some extent, the uncompromising intellectual quality of Tolstoy that so annoyed many of his contemporaries and has done much to persuade admirers of his fiction today to discount his theoretical writings was caused by the stubborn compulsion of his genius to think and to do things differently, to deviate always from accepted, conventional norms. The challenge of greatness left little room in his nature for humility before the greatness of others.

As Sir Isaiah Berlin has remarked, Tolstoy perceived with extraordinary clarity and penetration the total multiplicity of reality, yet he persisted in placing his faith in one vast unitary whole. This led him, in his tireless pursuit of truth, to search for absolutes in a world of gross uncertainty and erring men. And his inner need to achieve the ultimate in rational explanation often led him to push theory to the limits of absurdity, which he comes very close to doing in his views on history, education, and art. Yet the iconoclastic questions which his theories on these matters attempt to answer are nearly always profound and disturbing and compel the thoughtful reader to re-examine his own premises.

This is certainly true of the theories of *What Is Art?* For much of what he had to say in this book has a peculiar relevance nowadays when numerous so-called works of art would justify his findings in a very melancholy way. Counterfeit art he excoriated as pandering to the lowest taste, and with startling insight he predicted that it would eventually become the mass art of the future shamelessly exploited for commercial gain, a hideous menace to human sanity and culture. He clearly saw and condemned many abuses of art that have been attacked by progressive minds during the last few years, and his blistering repudiation of the middle-class cult of unintelligibility in art has frequently been echoed in our own times. If as a great literary artist he seemed to be wasting his time on mere criticism, he could jokingly pass off his early triumphs as the aberrations of youth. When an acquaintance remonstrated with him for not employing his artistic powers to create more such novels as *War and Peace*, he replied: "Why you know, that is just like the former admirers of some ancient French whore repeating to her: 'Oh, how adorably you used to sing chansonettes and flip up your petticoats.' "

Tolstoy's faith in the innate artistic instincts of the people, uniting them in a community of feeling making for the brotherhood of man, was a conviction later shared by Lenin. In fact, Soviet critics make much of the identity of their own position and Tolstoy's insistence that when art ceases to be art for all the people and caters only to the wealthy and educated it ceases to be necessary and important and becomes an empty amusement. That art should be accessible to all was Tolstoy's contention, but he also demanded that the artist must be entirely free to "infect" his audience with any feeling whatever—freedom was the core of Tolstoy's total thinking about the state of man.

Indeed, Tolstoy's image today in the Western world is largely identified with his God-given freedom to seek, mostly to seek for truth, whether the pursuit involved him in the complex lives of his imaginary men and women or in the controversial fields of religious, moral, political, or social thought. Truth, which in fiction had been Tolstoy's hero from the beginning, remained his hero to the end. For even after his conversion he never ceased to be a great realist in all questions related to art. His fiction marks the culmination of that development of Russian realism which began with Pushkin and included such great writers as Gogol, Turgenev, Dostoevsky, and Goncharov. Though Turgenev was known earlier in Western Europe, his works lacked the impact there of those of Dostoevsky and Tolstoy. By the turn of the second half of the nineteenth century, French realism had begun to drift in the direction of Flaubert's conception of impartiality and the scientific theories of Zola and his followers. In 1850 Flaubert had already begun to complain that French realists lacked a comprehension of the inner life, of the soul of things.

It was just this comprehension that Tolstoy possessed and it enabled him to extend the horizon of the tradition of realism which he had inherited. He perceived clearly that the inner truth of a novel must come from life itself. In the real world, where everything for him was part of existence, he saw the danger that realistic fiction would lose its connections with the great problems of life and degenerate into the dehumanization of art, into extremes of arid naturalism or excessive and meaningless formalism and symbolism. It was a measure of his integrity as a literary artist that after his conversion, the views of imaginary characters were presented with fidelity to the circumstances of their lives and the psychological truth of their personalities, even though they contradicted or disproved his own views.

If a valid test of realistic fiction, which is supposed to give a private view of those individual experiences which are the source of reality and truth, is the authenticity of its report, then Tolstoy's fiction must be regarded as among the most convincing in world literature. And if the timelessness and universality of appeal of imaginary men and women are taken as further tests, then Tolstoy's artistic accomplishment must again be singled out as supremely great, for his characters are as much alive today as ever, and among all classes of society, and in many countries.

To have life and meaning, remarked Galsworthy, art must emanate from one possessed by his subject, and Tolstoy's finest novels seem to convey this utter absorption on the part of their author. Much of our pleasure in reading his stories today arises from the feeling that our own sense of reality is enhanced and enriched by the workings of an imagination and perception that probe beneath the ordinary surface of life in an effort to explain the unknowable and clarify the obscure in the infinite complexity of human relations. This is reality immeasurably intensified, in which art becomes more real than nature and more living than life.

3

The European doctrine of natural law, which Tolstoy had become interested in as a young man, is the starting point of the philosophy of life that he developed in his old age. That is, all man's moral, aesthetic, and spiritual values are objective and eternal, and his inner harmony depends upon his correct relation to these values. By practical example and the advocacy of his writings he held forth to all the possibility of the establishment on earth of the Kingdom of God, that is, of truth and good. Though thousands of adherents set up organizations to carry out his beliefs, he discouraged any "church" in his name, learned to detest "Tolstoyans," and sadly admitted in the end that the spirit of stupidity as well as the spirit of God lived in every man. On the other hand, the Russian government regarded Tolstoy as a dangerous force in the body politic, but unwilling to risk international indignation by making a martyr of him, it allowed him to enjoy a kind of extra-territoriality on his estate at Yasnaya Polyana and contented itself with jailing his followers and forbidding his "treasonable" books and pamphlets to be published in Russia.

It is perhaps ironical that Tolstoy's beliefs, derived primarily from the teachings of Christianity, as well as from other great religions, are today frequently dismissed as of no consequence precisely by the Christian West. In the East, and especially in India, Tolstoy's beliefs seem still to be very much alive. Gandhi regarded himself as a humble follower, and his tremendously effective civil disobedience campaign stemmed in large measure from Tolstoy's teaching. And Sarvodaya, the mass movement today headed by Acharya Vinoba Bhave, a disciple of Gandhi, aims at the creation of a social order based on the Tolstoyan principle of love inspired by nonresistance or nonviolence. Though Tolstoy felt that the Japanese imitation of Western civilization would bring about their undoing, he prophesied a glorious future for the people of the Eastern world. In his "Letter to a Chinese" (1906), he wrote that "in our time a great revolution in the life of humanity will be accomplished, and in this revolution China ought to play a tremendous role at the head of the Eastern peoples."

Perhaps the doctrine that more than any other damaged his reputation as a thinker was that of nonresistance, which for Tolstoy meant that no physical force must be used to compel any man to do what he does not want to do or to make him desist from doing what he likes. Few visitors to Yasnaya Polyana failed to confront him with the obvious connundrums that arose out of such an extreme position. This was especially true of Americans, whose practical-mindedness and lack of spiritual qualities he criticized, although he was devoted to certain American thinkers and writers, such as Emerson, Thoreau, Whitman, William Lloyd Garrison, and Henry George, and he won a number of eager disciples in America. But it was the casual, curious American tourists who annoyed him: "It is just as though they had learned about me in a Baedeker and had come to confirm it," he once remarked of two of them. William Jennings Bryan, however, he admired as "an intelligent and religious American," but when the Great Commoner confronted him on the problem of nonresistance with the stock argument: What would he do if he saw a bandit murdering or violating a child, Tolstoy gave his stock answer, that in all his seventy-five years he had never met anywhere this fantastic brigand who would murder or outrage a child before his eyes, whereas in war millions of brigands kill with complete license.

In reality, Tolstoy, though adamant about the theory and the ends of his faith, was anything but dogmatic about the means of achieving them. He realized that the goal he set was often perfection, and though he might be uncompromising about it as a goal, he never expected men to attain it. "We search for mind, powers, goodness, perfection in all this," he wrote in his diary, "but perfection is not given to man in anything. . . ."

It is perhaps only in this limited sense of his doctrines, this striving through individual effort to achieve a more perfect world, that Tolstoy's philosophy can have any meaning for us at this time of international chaos. Like many thoughtful people today, he questioned whether human progress could be measured by its technical or scientific achievements or that modern civilization in general was moving toward the greater good. Progress, he insisted, does not consist of an increase in knowledge or in the material improvement of life. There can be progress only in a greater and greater understanding of the answers to the fundamental questions of life. A popular worship of scientific progress in a society still incapable of distinguishing between right and wrong represented a terrible danger to Tolstoy. He persistently denounced the notion that mankind can be made eternally happy and virtuous by rational and scientific means. "When the life of people is unmoral," he jotted down in his diary, "and their relations are not based on love, but on egoism, then all technical improvements, the increase of man's power over nature, steam, electricity, the telegraph, every machine, gunpowder, and dynamite, produce the impression of dangerous toys placed in the hands of children."

That governments in their systematic organization of society might logically strive to achieve righteousness, Tolstoy emphatically denied. When an American newspaper asked him in 1899 to comment on a proposal of the tsar for a "summit" conference of the great powers at The Hague to consider the question of disarmament in the interests of world peace, he replied: "My answer to your question is that peace can never be achieved by conferences or be decided by people who not only jabber, but who themselves go to war. . . . All such conferences can be summed up in a single dictum: All people are sons of God and brothers, and therefore they ought to love and not kill each other. Forgive my sharpness, but all these conferences invoke in me a strong feeling of disgust over the hypocrisy that is so obvious in them." The only tangible result of the Hague Conference was a series of conventions on the more "humane" conduct of war, and shortly after its conclusion the English plunged into a bloody struggle with the Boers.

The power that corrupts, Tolstoy asserted, was just as true of a democracy or a socialist state as of an absolute monarchy. For him political progress could not be measured in terms of democratic or socialist progress, for he saw in both the hypocrisy behind universal suffrage and the ever-present danger of power, even though held by the few elected by the many. His writings are full of warnings of the inevitability of both democratic and socialist states turning into monstrous dictatorships; of non-military democracies becoming powerful military states; of civilized countries championing fiendish theories of racial superiority; and of modern science being used to devise greater instruments of war to slaughter people more efficiently. All this, he foretold, will be achieved in the name of political, social, and scientific progress. And there will be no end of such "progress," he warned, as long as humanity continues to worship the law of men as higher than the law of God.

However one may regard Tolstoy's often highly original views, the various problems he wrote about have a striking relevance to burning issues today: the modernist movement in religion, war, peace and peace conferences, disarmament, underprivileged people, colonialism, capital punishment, governmental coercion, alcoholism, the perils of smoking, mass art, and nonviolence and civil disobedience in the Negro struggle for civil rights. Perhaps we have something to learn from his abrasive ideas and uncompromising stands on such matters. At least one thing we may learn is the little progress that has been made over the last sixty or more years in solving these problems. On the resolution of some of them the future of our civilization depends. A few of his solutions, which were ridiculed as hopeless Tolstoyan ideals in his own day, have ceased to be regarded as idealistic today.

Tolstoyism was in no sense the Moral Rearmament movement of its time. Any careful and systematic study of the whole of Tolstoy's thought reveals that he was fundamentally working within the concepts of nineteenth-century liberalism. Carried to its logical and perhaps utopian conclusion, such liberal thought inevitably results in the doctrine of Karl Marx or in the doctrine of Leo Tolstoy, for the end-product of both is a classless and stateless society. Marx sought to achieve his objective by revolutionary action based on a materialist approach to history which sanctioned the use of violence.

Tolstoy believed that the whole history of the last two thousand years had consisted essentially in the moral development of the masses and the demoralization of governments. He placed his faith in the moral development of the masses as a final answer to the universal oppression of the many by the few. For him, the progressive movement toward a classless and stateless condition of mankind depended upon the growing moral perfection of every individual through strict observance of the supreme law of love and the consequent repudiation of every form of violence. The West, with its incomplete liberalism today, condemns Soviet Marxism, but it has also decided that Tolstoy, though he may have diagnosed the disease of society correctly, has prescribed a kind of incantation for a cure. His way of love and moral perfection, we say, is impractical. On the other hand, we must now decide how practical is a hydrogen-bomb war to end all wars—or civilization.

However much of an incantation his remedy may have been, nevertheless there was a certain strength in Tolstoy's unworldliness from which we can perhaps learn something, for it enabled him to stand above the turmoil of everyday life and reach beyond history, beyond time itself, to find universal answers to the problems of living which are not conditioned by materialistic factors of human existence. Nor did the seer of Yasnaya Polyana ever lose his wonderful optimism. Returning home one day after seeing a beautiful sunset, he wrote in his diary: "No, this world is not a joke, and not a vale of trials or a transition to a better, everlasting world, but this world here is one of the eternal worlds that is beautiful, joyous, which we can and must make more beautiful and more joyous for those living with us and for those who will live in it after us."

SELECTED

BIBLIOGRAPHY

With the exception of a few of Tolstoy's writings on education, English translations of all the literary and non-literary works treated in this book may be found in numerous publications of individual and collected works. Though the complete works of Tolstoy have never been published in English, among the several editions of his collected works I would draw attention to what I consider the best such edition: *Tolstoy Centenary Edition*, translated by Louise and Aylmer Maude (21 vols.; London: Oxford University Press, 1928–37).

For a comprehensive listing of titles, in Russian and other languages, concerned with all aspects of Tolstoy's life and works, see "Bibliographical Survey" in the special limited edition of *Leo Tolstoy* by Ernest J. Simmons (Boston: Little, Brown and Company, 1946).

Below are a few biographical and critical studies in English of

Tolstoy's life and works that may serve the further interests
of readers of this book.

Abraham, Gerald. *Tolstoy*. London: Duckworth, 1935.

Bayley, John. *Tolstoy and the Novel*. London: Chatto and
Windus, 1966.

Berlin, Isaiah. *The Hedgehog and the Fox: An Essay on Tolstoy's
View of History*. London: Weidenfeld and Nicholson, 1954.

Christian, R. F. *Tolstoy's War and Peace*. London: Oxford, 1962.

Crauford, A. H. *The Religion and Ethics of Tolstoy*. London: Un-
win, 1912.

Fausset, H. I. *Tolstoy: The Inner Drama*. London: Jonathan Cape,
1927.

Gibbian, George. *Tolstoy and Shakespeare*. S. Gravenhage: Mouton & Co., 1957.

Gorky, Maxim. *Reminiscences of L. N. Tolstoy*. Translated by
S. S. Koteliansky and L. Woolf. New York: B. W. Huebsch,
1920.

Knight, G. Wilson. *Shakespeare and Tolstoy*. London: Oxford,
1934.

Lavrin, Janko. *Tolstoy: An Approach*. London: Methuen, 1948.

Lednicki, Waclaw. *Tolstoy Between War and Peace*. The Hague:
Mouton & Co., 1965.

Leon, Derrick. *Tolstoy: His Life and Work*. London: Routledge,
1944.

Lukács, George. *Studies in European Realism*. Translated by Edith
Bone. London: Hillway, 1950.

Maude, Aylmer. *The Life of Tolstoy*. 2 vols. *Tolstoy Centenary
Edition*. London: Oxford, 1929-30.

Nazaroff, A. I. *Tolstoy: The Inconstant Genius*. New York: Stokes,
1929.

Polner, Tikhon. *Tolstoy and His Wife*. Translated by Nicholas
Wredin. New York: Norton, 1945.

Rolland, Romain. *The Life of Tolstoy*. Translated by Bernard
Miall. New York: Dutton, 1911.

Simmons, Ernest J. *Leo Tolstoy*. Boston: Little, Brown and Company, 1946.

Steiner, E. A. *Tolstoy: The Man and His Message*. New York: F. H. Revell, 1908.

Steiner, George. *Tolstoy or Dostoevsky: An Essay in the Old Criticism*. New York: Knopf, 1959.

Tolstoy, Alexandra. *Tolstoy: A Life of My Father*. Translated by E. R. Hapgood. New York: Harper, 1953.

INDEX